Heart of a London Village

'We and our children shall pass away, but this Institution, based on such sound principles, and founded to promote such noble objects, shall not pass away.

Other voices will sound in these walls, other men will preside over and control its affairs, but rely upon it, that future generations will call us blessed for having founded, preserved, and handed down to them this Institution, and they in their turn will raise the prayer which now, with your sympathy and support I utter: "Esto Perpetua"'

Extract from the address given by Col. Wilkinson (President) on the occasion of the Institution's 50th Anniversary, February 1889.

First published 1991
by Historical Publications Ltd
32, Ellington Street, London N7 8PL
Telephone: 071–607 1628

on behalf of
The Highgate Literary and Scientific Institution
11 South Grove, Highgate, N6 6BS
Telephone: 081–340 3343

ISBN 0 948667 16 8

Typeset by Historical Publications Ltd
and Fakenham Photosetting, Fakenham
Printed by Biddles Ltd, Guildford, Surrey

All profits from the sale of this book
will go to the Institution's Development Fund

The illustration on the cover (also reproduced on pp24–25), shows Pond Square and Highgate High Street. The painting is by the daughter of the Village doctor, William Nathaniel Wetherell, who lived at No. 47 Highgate West Hill from 1771 – the house still exists. The doctor is shown as the horseman on the right. Church House may be seen immediately behind him; part of the buildings later taken over by the Institution are to the far right. In the High Street the Rose and Crown is to the foreground and behind that the inn sign of the White Lion at Nos. 64–66 may be seen. This inn closed in 1784, and therefore the dating of this picture as c1780 is probably correct. The small building in the centre of the picture with the triangular roof is the old Highgate lock-up, a short-term prison, which was about 7 foot square and 6 feet high.

Heart of a London Village

The Highgate Literary and Scientific Institution, 1839–1990

by members of
The Archives Committee
with a Foreword by Asa Briggs

Founded 1839

Published 1991
by Historical Publications Ltd
on behalf of
The Highgate Literary and Scientific
Institution

Acknowledgements

We wish to express our grateful thanks to:

ION TREWIN, JOAN SCHWITZER and VANESSA WHINNEY for their help and advice.

MRS BUTLER for a typing marathon.

JOHN PATEMAN for his research into the history of the Institution's Buildings.

PHILIP HOWARD for permission to reprint parts of his article in *The Times*.

JOHN RICHARDSON for permission to quote from *Highgate: its History since the Fifteenth Century* and *Highgate Past*, and for his very generous help with the printing and publication of this book.

The Estate of SIR JOHN BETJEMAN and JOHN MURRAY (PUBLISHERS) LTD, for permission to use an extract from John Betjeman's *Collected Poems* – 'Parliament Hill Fields'.

AND to the many members of this Institution who, over the years, have given so generously of their time and talents, without whom this book would not have been written.

Subscribers

(names as submitted)

Malcolm Abbs
Robert Adams
Mr T. and Professor D. Ades
Catherine H. Aitken
Mrs N.W.K. Anstiss
Ambrose and Ann Appelbe
Mohamed Aslam
T.F. Auber
Peter Barber
Sarah Barman
Neil Barnes
Dr Lilian A. Bates
R.E. Bay
Mr and Mrs Michael Baylis
John Bemrose
Pamela Benson
Ronald Bernstein
Miss Helen Betts
Hazel Block
John Boxall
R.M. Braithwaite
Lord Brimelow
Mrs K. Budgett-Meakin
Mrs Mary Burns
Mr and Mrs Ivor Burt
Mrs H.M. Butler
Mrs Sylvia Chalker
Esme Chandler
Mrs B. Colley
G.P. Cooper
Miss A. Cory-Wright
Susan Cox
Mrs Eva Crawley
D. Crane
Elizabeth Cunnington
Kay D. Curtis
S.R. Danos
C. David
D.F.A. Davidson
Ann Davies
Patricia Davies
M. Davis
Colin Donne
Cyril W. Downing
Gavin Doyle

Jean Duncan
Quentin Edwards
Miss R. Emms
R.H. and P. Farmer
E.M. Ferner
John Fielding
E.W. Fosbrook
Edward Fowler
Mrs P.M. Fox
J.G. Fraser
R.J. Freeman
Mrs J.M. Freeman
Mr and Mrs David Grant
M.M. Green
Sarah Grice
Miss V. Griffin
Mrs Beryl I.E. Gollance
Livia Gollancz
Oliver Gollancz
Pamela Griffiths
Dr Anne Grüneberg
Miss E.J. Guyatt
Martin G. Hamlyn
Ronnie Harris
May E.N. Hawkins
Mrs Diana Hayes
Thomas Hemsley
Mrs K.E. Hetherington
K.E. Hinrichsen
T.W.I. Hodgkinson
Mrs. G.W. Hogarth
Carol A. Howe
John R. Howe
Mrs Benita Horton
G.W.Y. Hucks
Pat Hutchinson
Miss M.E. Isaac
R.B. Jackson
Mrs Sally James
Cyril Jarvis
Christopher Johnson
Mrs D.M. Johnson
Nigel Johnson
C.R. Keeler
W.P. Kember

RICHARD P. KENNEDY
R.M. KIRK
PATRICIA KRELING
NORMA LACEY
JOHN LAKE
K.E. LEDDY
Dr BRIAN LODGE
HELEN LYNCH
T.G. LYTTELTON
CHARLOTTE McILWRAITH
LEONARD and SARAH MANASSEH
JOHN MANN
Mrs M. MÂSEK
J. MASSEY STEWART
S.W. MASSIL
C. MASON
D.L. MATHEWS
ADRIAN and KAIÀ MAYER
JAMES and SHEILAH MEIKLE
W. MENDELSSON
ELEANOR MARY MITCHELL
RICHARD MOLINEUX
ELISABETH MUNSON
JOAN NEALE
IAN V. ODDY
SHEELAGH O'KELLY
JOHN L. OLPHERT
Miss H.K. PALLAN
B. PALMER
FRANCES M. PARSONS
J.A. PATEMAN
D.A. PEARSON
Sir STANLEY and Lady PEART
KARIN PERRY
Miss L.K. PIKE
ROBIN S. PITMAN
M.A.R. POWERS
DORIS PRITCHARD
ISABEL RAPHAEL
SYLVIA READ
Sir JAMES REDMOND
MARIUS and MIMI REYNOLDS
B.L. RICHARDS
JOHN RICHARDSON
ANNE RIDDELL
TIM RIX
Dr. K.C. ROBINSON
A.K. RUSSELL

EDWARD RUSSELL
JENNY RUSSELL
FRANCES RUST
GABRIEL RYDER
JOHN SAMUEL
W. SANDERSON
MAT and JOAN SCHWITZER
JEAN SCOTT
DORIS SCHULER
Sir PATRICK SERGEANT
COLIN SHEAF
MARGARET and MICHAEL SHEAF
R.J. SIMMONS
ANN SMITH
Miss K. SMITH
DAVID and HAZEL SOLOMON
Dr. F. SOLOMON
JANET SONDHEIMER
Mrs B.C. STEPHENS
ISOBEL and MALCOLM STOKES
I.V.O. STOCKER
EDWARD SUTCLIFFE
Mrs P. SWIFT
K.W. SYKES
ALAN TAYLOR
RICHARD TAYLER
DONALD THACKERAY
Mrs M.I. TRAFFORD SMITH
Mrs K.V.A. THOMPSON
Mrs R.U. THONGER
B. URE
D. WAINWRIGHT
IAN WALLACE
ALISON WALEY
PETER WALTON
LINDA WARDEN
ALISON WATT
CHARLES WATTS-JONES
Mrs ETHEL WHETSON
KEN and VANESSA WHINNEY
JOHN H. WHITTLEY
JOHN WILKINSON
PHYLLIS WILLMOTT
ANTONY WILSON
Miss J.H. WILSON
A.M. WITHINGTON
E.R. YESCOMBE

CONTENTS

Foreword

Among the most interesting of Victorian local institutions, the Highgate Literary & Scientific Institution is outstanding. I was delighted, therefore, to be asked to write a brief foreword to this commemorative history.

The 150th anniversary of the Institution provides an opportunity not just to look back, but to look forward. It would be a magnificent testimony to the spirit of our own time, very different from that of 1840, if the Library could be modernised and the premises strengthened and repaired.

As President of the Victorian Society, I commend this project warmly, and as Chancellor of the Open University, I attach just as much importance to the lecture programme of the Institution, which is as lively as it ever was.

People living far away from Highgate will find this history of interest and of importance. Indeed, it is only through the assembling of such histories that we can develop a full understanding of the evolution of English culture.

ASA BRIGGS
Lord Briggs of Lewes F.B.A.
Provost of Worcester College, Oxford.

Introduction

Highgate – hive of history, home of poets Andrew Marvell, S.T. Coleridge, A.E. Housman and Sir John Betjeman and, so legend tells us, the resting place of Dick Whittington when summoned by Bow Bells, he turned again, into the City of London, to become its Lord Mayor.

Situated five miles from the City and Westminster on the summit of a steep ridge of hills, Highgate was from early times at an important road junction, a halting place for drovers on their way to Smithfield and where, during the Civil War, Royalists and Parliamentarians sought refuge and escape.

It was the sixteenth and seventeenth centuries that set a distinctive mark on Highgate. Attracted by the clean air and splendid views the aristocracy, gentry and well-to-do merchants built their second homes in Highgate. They provided employment for a large number of local people either working on the estates or in the houses or else supplying them with goods. In the seventeenth and eighteenth centuries many influential people who had links with the City came to live in Highgate. A number of wealthy merchants were non-conformists and Highgate had the religious advantage of being just outside the five mile limit within which, under the Act of 1665, non-conformists were prohibited from preaching.

'The nineteenth century brought the middle classes in force – the merchants, manufacturers, lawyers, civil servants and bankers, intent on a semi-rural life, taking advantage of the need of the old landowners to capitalise on their estates. Generally speaking Highgate has been middle-class ever since.' (*Highgate*, by John Richardson)

The heart of the village is the Highgate Literary & Scientific Institution – the Lit and Sci as it is familiarly called, or usually just 'The Institution'. Founded in 1839 it was part of the movement for self-improvement and enlightenment that spread over the whole country in the first part of the nineteenth century. Along with the learning and culture there has developed a strong social sense and neighbourliness that is typical of village society. Friendliness is a hallmark of the Institution and it shows itself in many ways: coffee and biscuits after lectures, parties, literary dinners, gossip and fun.

This book is not a straight historical narrative; it is made up of contributions by members of the Archives Committee. The chapters deal with different aspects of the Institution's activities – the Library, the lectures, archives and exhibitions. Inevitably it bears the mark of different hands, but it is hoped it will convey some of the enthusiasm which has enabled the Institution to surmount difficulties and survive for 150 years.

Vera Crane
Editor

The Archives Committee: Margaret Sheaf (Chairman), Rose Mary Braithwaite, Vera Crane, Elizabeth Cunnington, Gwynydd Gosling, Muriel Green, Frances Parsons, Jennifer Peters, Ann Riddell, O.B.E., Frances Rust, Christine Voss.

CHAPTER ONE

'To offer instruction'

A Short History of the Institution Movement

The Industrial Revolution of the 18th and 19th centuries set in train a movement for self-improvement among all classes of society. The spirit of enquiry generated by the new scientific inventions and their development in manufacturing processes led to the formation, originally in the big industrial cities of the north, of societies where members could attend lectures and have access to libraries. The first of these, the Manchester Literary and Philosophical Society, founded in 1781, and the Newcastle Literary and Philosophical Society, of 1793, were soon followed by similar organisations all over the country, as well as Mechanics' Institutions whose members included more working men. In 1826 the Society for the Diffusion of Useful Knowledge was formed, chaired by Lord Brougham, with the aim of spreading education to all classes.

There were also spontaneous efforts by the workers themselves; the earliest recorded institution had been the Spitalfields Mathematics Society of 1717, a mutual improvement society of weavers and other manual workers for the study of mathematics and experimental sciences. Later came the Brotherly Society of Birmingham (1796) and in 1794 the Cast Iron Philosophers, a group of artisans who worked in an iron foundry.

The main preoccupation was science and the Mechanics' Institutions had as their specific aim 'to offer instruction in the various branches of science which are of practical application to mechanics in their several trades, so that they may the better comprehend the reason for each individual operation that passes through their hands...There is no trade which does not depend more or less on scientific principles: to teach what these are and to point out their practical application will form the basis of the establishment' (Edinburgh School of Arts, founded 1821, later to become the Heriot-Watt College).

The London Mechanics' Institution, founded in 1823, was the real starting point of the Mechanics' Institution movement in England. Resolution 6 in its Constitution may serve as a blue-print: 'Among the objects which the London Institution shall have especially in view shall be the establishment of lectureships on the different arts and sciences, a library of reference and circulation, a reading room, a museum of models, a school of design and an experimental workshop and laboratory'. To avoid controversy politics and religion were banned. The library and reading room were focal points and even the smallest institution seldom failed to set up a library.

By 1825 seventy new institutions had been founded; at the same time other institutions similar in character – Mechanics' and Apprentices' Libraries, Mutual Improvement Societies and the more middle-class Literary and Scientific Institutions were springing up.

By 1841 the number of all types had risen to 305 and by 1851, the year of the Great Exhibition, the number had more than doubled to 698. With little or no division between the two main types of institution the term 'Literary and Scientific' began to be widely used as an alternative to Mechanics' Institution. The Mechanics' Institution at Hackney changed its name to the new title – 'Finding that 'mechanic' was a stumbling block we struck out the word'.

To keep up their membership all societies had to popularise their activities. Systematic science courses gave way to miscellaneous subjects such as popular science, literature, music, history and travel. In libraries scientific textbooks came to be outnumbered by works of fiction, travel and general literature. Reference rooms were converted into rooms displaying newspapers. Exhibitions became fashionable and generally very profitable. The need for this kind of development was succinctly put by the President of the Manchester Mechanics' Institute – 'The great point, I am convinced, is to combine more of what will be felt as relaxation with our communication of knowledge. After a day of hard work a man wants refreshment and ease.'

The movement reached its peak around the 1860s. With the Public Libraries Act of 1850 many institution libraries were eventually taken over to form the nucleus of the public library system. Further erosion followed the Education Acts of 1870 and 1902 and the Technical Instruction Act of 1889 meant that the need for some of the Institutions' educational functions had been superseded.

Of those Institutions which are still active, twelve, including The Highgate Literary & Scientific Institution, in 1989 formed the Association of Independent Libraries for the exchange of information on questions of mutual interest.

CHAPTER TWO

'To excite and cultivate...'

Foundation and Terms of Reference of The Highgate Literary & Scientific Institution

On 16 January 1839 an Inaugural Meeting was called by Harry Chester at the Gate House Tavern in Highgate Village 'For the purpose of forming an Institution designed to excite and cultivate an intelligent interest in the objects of Literature and Science'. Seventy-six residents responded to the call by Harry Chester, Clerk to the Privy Council, and put down their names to become members of the new Highgate Literary & Scientific Institution. They were people with private means, professional men and local shop-keepers; artisans were also to be encouraged to join. Since 1822 there had been a Book Club in Highgate, which met monthly in members' houses, but that was only for 'gentlemen' – no-one in trade was permitted to join. The Institution was intended for all classes.

In its first set of rules the Institution set out:

'To create and foster a taste for reading and a taste for intellectual pursuits – to bring within reach of Artisan and Mechanic those mental enjoyments which next to the consolations of religion and the blessings of natural affection are the best friends to Virtue and Happiness. To offer books, not only in the rooms of the Institution, but at the firesides of Members and Associates – and lectures to stimulate and gratify an intelligent desire for information. Above all to unite all classes and all parties in one common object – the general good of themselves and all around them'.

The founder of the Institution made this proud boast in his Inaugural Address: 'In this hamlet at least no one endowed by Providence with reason can from henceforth be grossly ignorant except by his own wilful default'.

1. Invitation card for the meeting to inaugurate the Highgate Literary & Scientific Institution on January 16, 1839 at the Gate House Tavern on the corner of West Hill and North Road. The Chair was taken by Harry Chester, who was elected the first President.

2. The Gate House Tavern, scene of the inaugural meeting of the HLSI. Watercolour by H.G. Hine from the Highgate Horn Boke *(1846).*

A MEETING

WILL BE HELD AT THE

GATE HOUSE, IN HIGHGATE,

On Wednesday Evening, Jan. 16, 1839,

FOR THE PURPOSE OF FORMING AN

INSTITUTION

Designed to excite and cultivate an intelligent interest in the objects of
LITERATURE AND SCIENCE.

THE CHAIR WILL BE TAKEN AT EIGHT O'CLOCK PRECISELY.

CHAPTER THREE

'Buildings in the Square'

The Institution's Buildings
– a Reconstruction

The Institution stands in the centre of Highgate, facing Pond Square and, at the back, from the top of Swain's Lane, looks down over the London sky-line.

As Philip Howard wrote in his article in *The Times* of 17 November 1990: 'From up there you can see the whole of London spread out before your feet like a magical Persian carpet. You feel that you could stride across it in one seven-league step to the Weald of Kent 20 miles away. And look – there's the Barbican – or is it? Certainly, there beneath your feet is the dome of St Paul's still glittering like a great bubble over its city. But if you look north from benighted Wapping, you can see the lights twinkling up on Highgate Hill – the lights of the village that refused to be swallowed up by the all-devouring metropolis.'

The Institution owns a group of buildings in South Grove. No. 11 and the Cottage attached to it are listed buildings in Group II; 10A is listed in Group II*. The Institution uses only No. 11 for its own activities. No. 10A is leased to the Highgate Society, and the Cottage and a group of garages at the rear are also let.

The history of these buildings is not known for certain, but John Pateman's research, at the end of this chapter, throws new light on their origins. In the mid-seventeenth century there had been three, or perhaps four, cottages on the site disposed round a well. On the ground occupied by two of the cottages Church House (No. 10 South Grove) was built in 1752 by Peter Storer, brother-in-law of Sir John Hawkins, the friend and biographer of Dr Samuel Johnson. A coach-house and stables were built alongside to the west.

The Institution had begun its life in two rented rooms at No. 1 Southwood Terrace, Southwood Lane, and moved to its present home in 1840, about a year after its founding. At that time Leopold Neumegen was running a Jewish School from Church House, which he had on lease from the Hawkins family. Not requiring the coach-house and stables belonging to Church House he sub-let them to the new Institution. These became No. 11 South Grove. The ground floor was turned into a Library at the front; the large coach-house at the back became the Lecture Hall and in the centre, off a

courtyard, was the Committee Room; upstairs was accommodation for the Librarian. A further building, No. 10A, between 11 South Grove and Church House, was erected by the School in 1848. Between the Wars 10A was used by the 1919 Club for Domestic Servants; during the 2nd World War it was used as a studio by Margaret Thomas, R.A. Subsequently it was used as a handbag warehouse until in 1966 it was leased to the newly-formed Highgate Society. In 1851 the Lecture Hall (the present Library) underwent a grand refurbishment; raked seating was put in and a new platform and diagram board provided for the use of lecturers. Lord Shaftesbury, the famous philanthropist, was the guest of honour at the re-opening ceremony.

In 1879, forty years after its founding, the Institution embarked on an ambitious scheme of improvement. The open courtyard was roofed in and made into the Lecture Hall; the former Lecture Hall became the Library; the former Library was panelled and became the Reading Room; an entrance porch and lobby were constructed (these were restored in 1988); and the living accommodation was modernised. Baroness Burdett-Coutts opened the new Lecture Hall in 1880.

The freehold of the Institution's original premises, which had been held on successive leases from the Hawkins family, was acquired in 1932 for £1700 after protracted negotiations. In 1936 the Institution bought from the Hawkins trustees an additional property consisting of Church House, No.

3. Thompson's map of St Pancras Parish, c1800, Highgate section. Two large ponds are in what is now Pond Square.

4. Highgate Old Ponds in the centre of the Village: a view from the Institution. Pencil drawing by Henry Scrimgeour, 1852. The ponds were filled in in 1869.

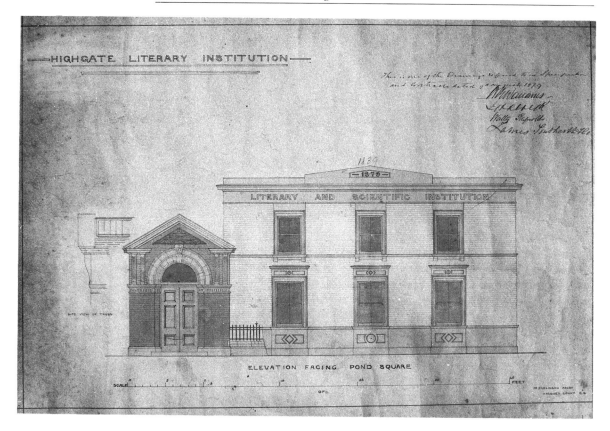

5. Plan of the proposed
new frontage of the
Institution by
Rawlinson Parkinson,
1879.

6. Plan of the new
Hall of the Institution
by Rawlinson
Parkinson, 1879.

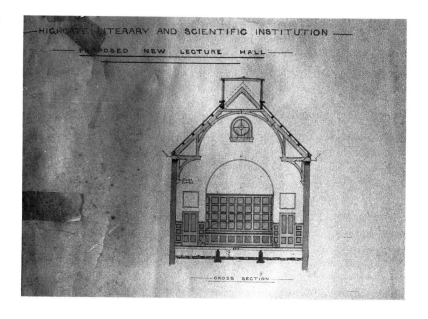

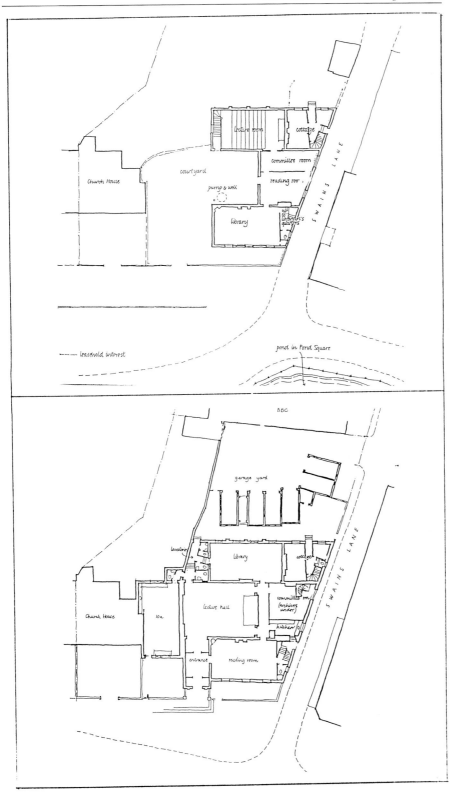

7. A plan of the Institution buildings, 1840, drawn by Jim Peters for the 1989 **Heart of a London Village** *Exhibition. The Institution spent about £400 on converting its newly acquired buildings, but this included renovations and furnishings. The back room (assumed to have been the coachhouse) was equipped with tiered seating with no backs and the average attendance of over 100 at lectures must have been a tight squeeze. The front room (probably stables with loft over) was equipped as a library and museum, and the Librarian was accommodated on the first floor, which provided four bedrooms, living room and dining room. There was a small reading room next to the committee room.*

8. A plan of the Institution buildings, 1989, drawn by Jim Peters for the 1989 **Heart of a London Village** *Exhibition. In 1957 Church House with some land was sold, but not the yard, on which the present garages were built. In 1982, thanks to generous help from Colonel John Hines, the Institution was able at last to build proper lavatories, to modernise the Cottage, and to convert the cellars for much needed archive space.*

10A and a shop and garage at the back of No. 11. The cost was £2019. The property was bought 'partly as a contribution towards the preservation of the amenities of Highgate Village' and partly with an eye to future needs and expansion of the Institution.

Church House was let and, because of the intervention of World War II, never used for the Institution's own activities. When in 1955 it needed extensive repairs and modernisation for which the Institution did not have funds, it was put on the market and eventually sold in 1957 for £4600. No. 10A, the shop and yard were retained and in 1958 six lock-up garages were built, at a cost of £1873, on the site of the shop and yard. These buildings, together with Institution Cottage, have proved a valuable investment.

John Pateman has recently been researching the history of the site and has summarised his findings so far:

When were the buildings which now house the Institution erected? What was there before them? These are questions which, surprisingly, have never been seriously investigated; and it has to be admitted at the outset that what follows here is often speculation rather than established fact. It may however highlight some of the problems and grey areas and perhaps prompt a more thorough and scholarly investigation by others.

The feature in the Institution which attracts the knowing eye is the brick vaulted cellar and the stairway which leads from it to a trap-door in the floor of the Lecture Hall. The cellar is now the Archive Room and its roof has been so much restored and so well painted over that no-one is prepared to venture a firm opinion on its age; but it would certainly seem to be too impressive a structure to have belonged to a simple cottage. The stairway however has been pronounced by several authorities to be of possibly Jacobean or even Tudor origin. Ignoring its period, for what purpose are we to suppose it was built? Bearing in mind that the outlet of the stairway was until 1880 into an open yard, could it have been for anything but an inn? The northern end of Swain's Lane would have been a likely site for an inn; at the top of a steep hill it is on one of the three routes to and from the City of London, at the base of the Village Green Triangle, and facing the Ponds.

The informative chapter and appendix on Inns in John Richardson's *Highgate: Its History since the Fifteenth Century* has no mention of an inn on this site but says that in 1552, when licensing by the Justices began, there were already five inns in the Village, the names of which are not given in the records. 'Our' inn would have had to be of, or near to, this period since we believe that we can trace what was on the site from the early seventeenth century. The *Survey of London* Vol XVII (1936), p38 refers to a tradition, which it discredits, that the Institution was erected on the site of the 'Cow and Hare'. There are no details given of the origin of the tradition. John Richardson's book (pp16 and 150) mentions an inn which fits most of our requirements and which it would be exciting to be able to claim. Known as 'le Swan', it is the earliest known alehouse in Highgate, appearing in the

Cantelowes Court Rolls of 1480 – but not after 1536. Concerning its location we read: 'The triangular village green was bounded by the High Street and what became The Grove and South Grove…There were houses on or by the green in the fifteenth century according to the Court Rolls. One was called le Swan, probably an inn…'; and later, 'Its location was Highgate Hill'.

If we move forward to the second half of the seventeenth century, we find that in 1662, or soon after, John Storer, clerk, unwilling to accept the Act of Uniformity of 1662 and realising that preferment in the Church was now at an end for him, came to Highgate and in 1672 obtained a licence to keep a school. Nothing appears to be known of any school he may have kept and little more about his time in Highgate. He and his elder son, also John, seem gradually to have acquired possession of three cottages (6,6,1 on Illustration 9), one of which (1) they surrendered in 1678 to Robert Massey, a joiner, on condition that he did not erect any building 'to the prejudice of them or obstruction of their view.' (The numbering on Illustration 9 is referred to throughout the rest of this article.) The two Storers secured themselves further in 1689 by obtaining a parcel of land in front of their house (8). This

9. The buildings on the Institution site.

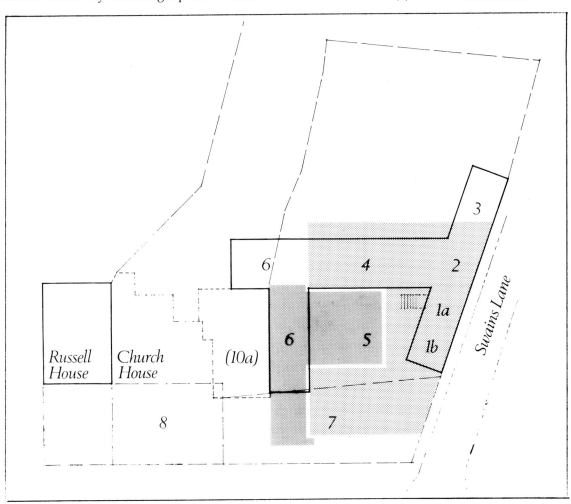

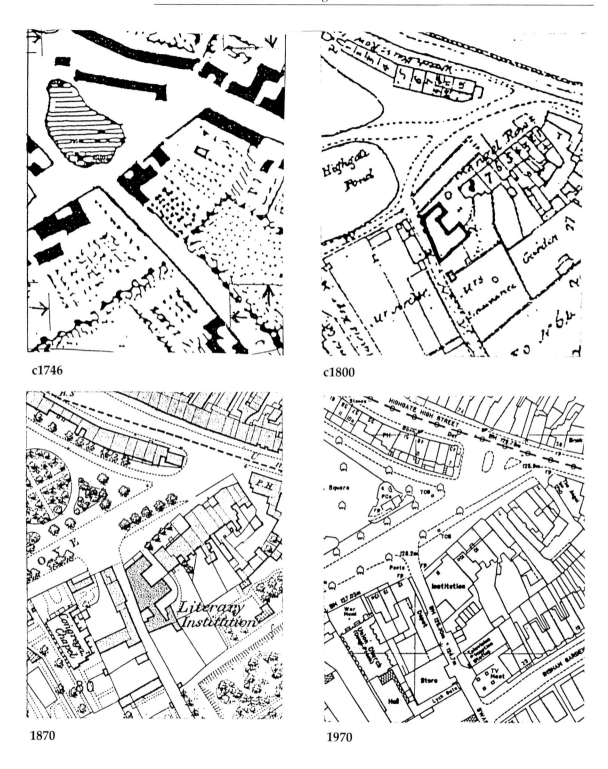

c1746

c1800

1870

1970

10. The corner of Swains Lane and South Grove as depicted on maps from c1746 to 1970.

interpretation of a complicated passage in the *Survey* (p35) is supported by Rocque's map of *c*1746, which may appear roughly drawn and the detail imprecise, and the measurements for which were obtained by pacing them out. Nevertheless he is known to have recorded with a broad accuracy buildings in Highgate and the City of London which are no longer there. In what follows Rocque has usually been followed wherever there has been doubt.

In July 1658 Merrell White, spinster, acquired a messuage (a dwelling place with the outbuildings and land, if any, attached thereto), yard and garden in Swain's Lane. The vendor was Sir Robert Payne who at one time or another held property east of Swain's Lane as well as a tenure of Arundel House and Dorchester House before landing in gaol just before his death in 1658. We think this was the property (3) shown south of Institution Cottage on Rocque's map. In March 1661 Merrell White bought a second property in Swain's Lane (2).

A prominent figure in the next two decades – for our story – was John Welbe of Whitechapel, gentleman and grocer, and son-in-law of Robert Massey. In August 1682 he bought from Massey the messuage (1) which Massey had acquired from the Storers in 1678; and the following year, 1683, Merrell White (now Mrs Hugh Dorrell) sold him the cottage next door (2). In 1683 Welbe also came by a strip of waste (7) measuring 60' east to west, 30' at Swain's Lane end and 22' at the other. The strip is now almost entirely taken up by the present Reading Room.

In 1692 Welbe sold cottage (2) to Mark Wynn, a carpenter, and a little later divided the next door cottage (1) into two (1a and 1b), both being entitled to use the well and pump in the Yard (5). On Welbe's death in 1697 the two cottages passed to his widow and on her death to their daughter Mary. Mary married Joseph Hurt and in 1711 they sold the cottages to William Brown with the same stipulation as had been imposed on Robert Massey in 1678, namely that no building should be erected 'to the prejudice of them or obstruction of their view'.

Welbe's other holding (2) which, it will be recalled, had been bought by Mark Wynn, passed on his death to his son, John. When John died in 1730 he left in trust for his mother, who had remarried, not only the Cottage but also a coachhouse and stables. These can only have been built on the waste ground (4) in front of the cottage – a view supported by the Court Rolls quoted in the *Survey* (p37). It is possible that the coachhouse and stables were a single double-storeyed building with the coachhouse below and the stables above. This was not an unusual arrangement especially when, as in this case, the slope of the ground encouraged it; and it has to be remembered that at the time the ground south of today's Library had not been built up but followed the gradient of Swain's Lane. When excavations were being dug recently prior to the building of a Library Annexe, the wall at the south-east corner of the Library was found to go down nine feet below floor level.

We must now return to the Storer family, the first of whom came to Highgate *c*1670 and gradually assembled a sizeable home (6). This came in 1717 to Peter Storer, grandson of the first John Storer. Peter added to his

11. Watercolour of Highgate High Street and Pond Square, c1780. Behind the horseman on the right can be seen Church House, and adjoining it is its stable and coachhouse which in 1840 became the HLSI.

estate in 1736 by purchasing from the executors of the Wynn Trust the Cottage (2) together with the coachhouse and stables (4), a garden and some waste ground. When he died in 1749 he left to his son, also Peter, a 'capital messuage (21 May 1717) and a parcel of waste before' (8). If the date in brackets which forms part of the entry in the Court Rolls is taken at face value, it has relevance to the date when the present Church House was built. This will be looked at more fully later. The inheritance did, of course, include the Messuage (2) with coachhouse and stables (4) acquired in 1736.

In 1752 the younger Peter Storer bought from the great-grandson of William Brown the two Cottages (1a and 1b) and thus became the owner of the whole site presently occupied by Church House, the Institution (including 10A) and Institution Cottage.

Peter Storer lived and died a bachelor. He was a wealthy man, as can be seen from the many substantial bequests in his will. He lived in style 'with an unencumbered landed property of £2,000 p.a.' and kept six carriage horses. According to his niece he was a kind and affectionate man, being particularly devoted to his sister Sidney who married John Hawkins in 1753, and to his horses. He was perhaps fond too of Mary Russell 'then living with him', and in his will left her £3,000 Bank Stock and £300 'as a grateful acknowledgement', he wrote in the will, 'of her unwearied care and diligence in nursing both my mother and myself to the prejudice of her own health and reputation'. But we fancy that there were times when he wearied of the all-female company in the family home and for that reason converted the Cottage (2) into a comfortable bachelor establishment into which he could escape and from which there was ready access to the adjoining stables (4). There remain, we like to think, two reminders of his sojourn in the cottage – the extremely good fielded panelling of c1700 and the cupboard with the three purposeless stairs, except that they could have provided the communication to the upper-storey stables. Both are on the first floor and both have so far baffled enquirers.

It was almost certainly Peter Storer too who converted the adjoining Cottages (1a and 1b) to stables between 1752, when he gained possession of them, and his death in 1759. His coachhouse could accommodate his mother's carriage and Mary Russell's no doubt, but it may have been better for there to be separate stabling for the horses!

Peter Storer died on 8 August 1759 and the *Survey* (p36) records that 'Thus Church House came into the possession of its best known owner, John Hawkins, in right of his wife'. This seems a clear assertion that the Church House of today existed in 1759.

Although the history of Church House does not strictly fall within the compass of this narrative, it may be excusable briefly to consider when it was built. In siting the Storers' home where we did in the diagram (6) we were guided by two considerations: Rocque's map demanded it; and it seemed the only siting which would bring coherence to the many individual pieces of information in the *Survey* and the Court Rolls. The shape and location of the Storer home as we picture it, does not coincide at all with the 1991 Church House nor could the former have become the latter by conversion. There must have been at some stage a pulling-down and a rebuilding.

It has been remarked earlier that the Court Rolls and the *Survey* are firm that the capital messuage inherited by the younger Peter Storer in 1751 was the one inherited by his father in 1717. We have to conclude therefore that the present Church House was, like the stables on the site of the cottages (1a and 1b), erected by the younger Peter Storer between 1751 and 1759.

Neither Sir John Hawkins nor his descendants are thought to have lived much, if at all, in Church House; and the property was almost continuously let. On 22 April 1782, for instance, Sir John was granted licence to lease for 21 years:

'A messuage (Church House)
Coachhouses and Stables (1 and 4) adjoining a Yard (5)
and garden behind
a small messuage behind the said coachhouses and stables heretofore in the tenure of John Walklin (a gardener) and now of Cornelius.'

The above extract from the Court Rolls is interesting for several reasons: it sets out in detail the extent of the property in 1782; the word 'coachhouses' in the plural would seem to justify our relating it both to (1) and (4). It may provoke surprise that a gardener should have lived for a period in the cottage (2) of his former employer. This is not so surprising if it is realised that Walklin was highly thought of by Peter Storer, who left him £100 in his will.

Sir John Hawkins died in 1789 and his wife, Sidney, was admitted to:

A capital messuage (Church House) with waste before and garden behind
A messuage lately erected heretofore in the occupation of John Walklin
Ground which abuts south on a garden...and had formerly standing thereon a messuage (2), coachhouse (4) and a parcel of waste (premises purchased by Peter Storer in 1736)
Land adjoining the house heretofore of Peter Storer the younger (2)
Coachhouse and Stable before (1a and 1b) and waste (60' x 30' x 22'), on which ground stood formerly two messuages heretofore the estate of William Brown.

If this extract is read in conjunction with that in the previous paragraph, it can be accepted that in 1789 Church House was still standing; that the cottage (2) in which the younger Peter Storer and his gardener had lived, had just been substantially, if not completely, rebuilt: that the coachhouse and stables (4) must have become derelict, as they are omitted from the list; and that the stabling (1a and 1b) still stood.

In 1794 when J.S. Hawkins was admitted on his mother's death, the property was as it had been five years earlier except that the stabling (1a and 1b) may have gone. There remained only Church House, Institution Cottage and land. In the map of *c*1800, however, the buildings on the site of what is now No. 11 South Grove coincide almost exactly with the present Institution buildings, if one allows for the 1880 Lecture Hall on the site of the Yard. From this we can reason that the buildings which appeared on the site of the present Reading Room, Kitchen, Committee Room, Library and Librarian's quarters were erected between 1794 and *c*1800, probably nearer the earlier rather than the later date for the following reason. There is in the Institution a watercolour of South Grove in which the Reading room is clearly recognisable. The date of the painting has been given as *c*1780, which is no longer now tenable, as the earliest date for the Reading Room is 1795; but the nearer to 1795 the date is put, the more probable it is.

Information about the buildings is sparse from 1800 to 1840. Bryan Hurwitz, a Polish Jew and sometime Professor of Hebrew in the University of London, moved into Church House in 1802 and from there ran a school for Jewish boys and girls, some of them boarders. Needing additional space in 1810 he leased Russell House for a year or two; whether he expanded at any stage into the future No. 11 South Grove is not known, but it is not unlikely, for in 1821 prior to handing over the school to Leopold Neumegen, he negotiated a 21-year lease of those premises. Neumegen still held the lease in 1839 and it was with him that the Institution treated for a sub-let towards the end of that year. A rental of £40 p.a. was agreed, the Committee of Management happy in the expectation that £15 could probably be recouped by letting Institution Cottage.

The cost of adapting the new premises for the purposes of the Institution and providing the necessary fittings and furniture was estimated in January 1840 to be about £250. In March it was £322. The actual cost proved in July to be £382. It was thought to be worth it, as the President, Harry Chester, made clear in his address at the formal opening on 12 May 1840. He said: 'Heretofore lodgers we are now householders and settled in a comfortable home. Instead of the little Reading Room in Southwood Terrace we have in this building a comfortable Reading Room of good dimensions…The building which you now occupy, has undergone some curious transformations in its time and been applied to very dissimilar purposes; but I am sure you will pronounce that it has been skilfully and successfully adapted to the purpose to which it is now appropriated'. If only Harry Chester could have gone into more detail!

As it is, the only information available on the disposition of the accommodation comes from addresses by two sometime Presidents of the Institution, Col. Wilkinson and W.P. Bodkin. Speaking in 1866 and 1868 respectively they both agree that the ground floor comprised four apartments, viz. Theatre; Committee room; Assistant Secretary/Librarian's Room; Library. Contrary to the comfortable words of Harry Chester in 1840 there seems to have been no Reading Room 26 and 28 years later. A Minute in 1839 records that a suggestion was made during a meeting of the Management Committee that the Committee Room might be kept open longer for the reading of newspapers. From this it would appear that the Committee Room was also the Reading Room. Of the other apartments the Theatre was situated in what is now the Library. A drawing dated May 1851 shows a room filled with steeply rising rows of benches, lit by a central chandelier and with niches in the south wall containing busts of famous people. For the lecturer there was a blackboard fitted to the west wall. The small windows high up on the south wall were put in *c*1850. The Theatre served also as a classroom.

Today's Reading Room housed the Library and Museum. The Assistant Secretary/Librarian worked from the present Kitchen, it is assumed, though some say that his office was the southern half of today's Committee Room, and the rest of that room was joined up with the Kitchen to provide a more spacious, if darker, Reading Room-cum-Committee Room. Nothing of substance is known of the layout of the Librarian's apartment on the upper floor. From a Minute of November 1883 there appears to have been a kitchen, although the Librarian of 1939 had to use the main kitchen on the ground floor and the table top in that room also concealed the bath.

What is known and from surer evidence is that Librarians and Committees of Management have been subject from the very beginning to much the same tribulation, as the following extracts from Minute Books make clear.

June 1845: Outer wall in a dilapidated state.

October 1851: Rain coming through the roof into two upstairs bedrooms. Gas escaping.

June 1853: Urgent repairs needed to the Cellar. Costs to be kept to a minimum.

March 1860: Repairs in Librarian's quarters to cost £26.9.0d plus a further £2 for battening the walls in one room to prevent the damp.

May 1865: Blocked spouts causing influx of water over ceilings and the depression of both ceilings and floors.

March 1866: State of part of the roof, the pipes and gutters such as to cause water to pour into the sleeping apartments, drenching walls and penetrating to walls below.

Ironically, while there was an abundance of unwanted water, domestic water had to be drawn from the well and with the pump in the courtyard. Mains water did not reach North London until 1846. Institution Cottage had to wait a further three years and the tenant had to pay the full cost of the installation.

In 1848 a new building, now No. 10A South Grove, was erected between the Institution and Church House. Neumegen, we read, went bankrupt in 1843, the Jewish school moved to Brighton and Kilham Roberts moved into Church House, where he started an academy. For some reason he decided to vacate Church House and build new school accommodation on the waste land between Church House and the Institution. The Management Committee were business-like in their dealings with Roberts, detailing precisely the dimensions of the west wall of the proposed new building and demanding 'the right of raising it or otherwise and placing a roof thereon to enclose the recess in order to form a Lecture Room'. Further, the wall was to be of the thickness to allow this. It is noteworthy that the Institution had this project in mind as early as 1847.

During the course of a lengthy address in October 1869 Col. Wilkinson said: 'Highgate with all its wealth and enterprise still lacks a building properly fitted to accommodate such a Society as this'. Ten years were to pass before anything happened, and this was not surprising as the Institution came near to closing during that period. Eventually the architect, Rawlinson Parkinson, who was a member of the Institution, was asked to draw up plans

a) for the erection of a new Lecture Theatre over the courtyard capable of seating 300 persons;

b) to adapt the present Theatre for the purpose of a Library and to provide a good classroom;

c) to panel the ceiling of the Reading Room, re-glaze the windows with plate glass, and provide comfortable seats for readers;

d) to construct a handsome porch and corridor by which both Reading Room and Theatre will be approached;

e) to add three windows to the first floor and raise the pediment which will greatly improve the present,mean appearance of the front elevation.

If one looks now at the north elevation of the upper storey, it becomes apparent that pre–1880 there were no windows looking on to Pond Square – a fact which supports the view that when this part of the Institution was built *c*1795, it was built as stabling with the upper storey a loft. To Parkinson's brief there were shortly added further instructions, viz.

f) the whole building to be re-roofed;

g) the Swain's Lane wall, being porous, to be cemented over;

h) the Reading Room floor joists and many of the floor boards, being rotten, to be replaced;

i) a wall to be built at the east end of the new Theatre to satisfy the lessee of 10A (it appears that he was not bound by the agreement made with Kilham Roberts).

Finally, allowance had to be made in costing the project for renovations in the Librarian's quarters, for repairs in Institution Cottage and for furniture and fittings in the new Theatre itself. Messrs Southcott's tender, the lowest submitted, which after paring started at £1106, ended at £1750. The work was completed early in 1880 and the new Theatre formally opened by Baroness Burdett-Coutts in March 1880.

Thereafter, the first important occurrence was the purchase in 1932 of the freehold of 11 South Grove and Institution Cottage for £1600. In 1937 a further £2019 was laid out for 10 and 10A South Grove and for sundry small buildings and land to the south 'in view of the possible extension of the premises'. The premises were not extended. Church House was sold in 1957. 10A has been let out continuously since it was acquired, as has Institution Cottage except for a brief period in the 1980s. Institution Cottage now is elegantly decorated and furnished and enjoys many of the modern conveniences; but it has not long been like this. In 1981, when occupied by Mrs Chitty from whom the cottage derives its official designation of 'Chitty's Cottage', it was still lit by gas, had no indoor lavatory or bathroom, and but one cold water tap. The hardy Mrs Chitty was the widow of one of the last of the Village's stonemasons who had first come into prominence with the foundation of Highgate Cemetery in 1839. But the Cottage still has, as reminders of Peter Storer, the panelling and the cupboard with the purposeless stairs.

SOURCES

The Survey of London, Vol. XVII (1936).
Highgate: Its History since the Fifteenth Century, by John Richardson (1983).
Extracts from Cantelowes Court Rolls.
Minutes of H.L.S.I. Management Committee meetings.
H.L.S.I. archives.
Material supplied by J.S. Peters for the Institution's Sesquicentenary.

CHAPTER FOUR

Members and Money

The story of an Institution is in large part told by the figures of membership and finances, and those of the H.L.S.I. certainly trace its ups and downs.

At the Inaugural Meeting on 16 January 1839, seventy-six residents of Highgate put their names down to join the new Institution, and by the end of the year there were 110 members. During the first forty years of the Institution's existence membership was around 200; then, following the great building programme of 1879, it rose over ten years to 700, a figure not reached again until 1971. Membership increased strongly in the 1980s to about 1450 at the end of 1990. In that year there were two principal categories of member: Ordinary (i.e. single) and Household (which included children under 21 living at home).'Other' included Honorary members, and residents of retirement homes in Highgate who paid a reduced rate of subscription. The numbers at the end of 1990 were: Ordinary 387, Household 1050 (350 subscribers) and Other 18.

The Institution set out in 1839 to provide for all classes, with some success. In 1848, for instance, there were

9	Life or Honorary members
121	Annual members (106 of them male)
71	Associates (including spouse and children of members)
36	Laborers (*sic*) and Mechanics
	a total of 237

The number of 'Laborers and Mechanics', later renamed 'Associates 2nd Class (working men)', dwindled away until the 1870s, when the closing of the Working Men's Club brought in more members and the number rose to 49. Again there was a slow falling off, and the category finally disappeared from the records in 1922.

The pattern of membership has changed considerably since the early years. Now more than half the members are female; and whereas, when Highgate Village had a country setting, virtually all the members lived close by, nowadays about a fifth live more than two kilometres from the Institution, and twenty have moved well away from London, but maintain their membership.

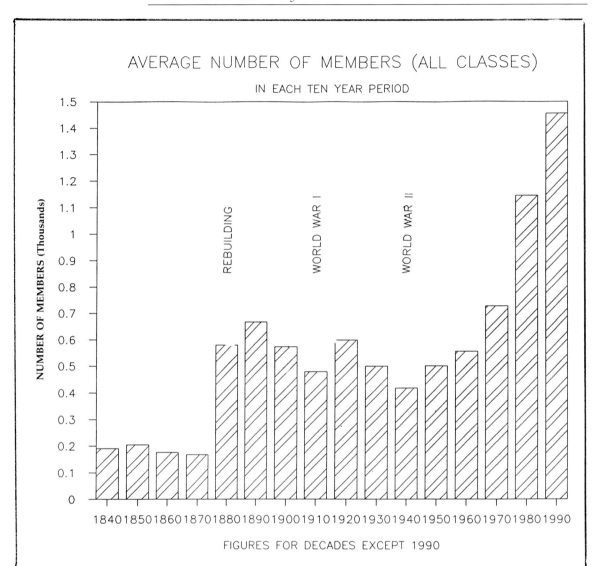

AVERAGE NUMBER OF MEMBERS (ALL CLASSES)

IN EACH TEN YEAR PERIOD

Account of Receipts and Payments of the Highgate Literary and Scientific Institution
Dr. for the Year 1849. **Cr.**

	£. s. d.		£. s. d.
To Balance due to the Institution, 1st January, 1849	9 16 2½	By Expences of Lectures, including Commission and Atten-	
,, Subscriptions of Members and Associates............	152 15 0	dance	9 18 2
,, ,, of Laborers and Mechanics............	3 7 0	,, ,, Musical and other Entertainments	25 8 0
,, Sale of Tickets to Lectures	5 12 0	,, ,, Shaksperian Readings..................	12 8 4
,, ,, Musical Entertainments, &c............	23 14 6	,, Rent, Rates and Taxes, and Insurance	65 1 6
,, ,, Shaksperian Readings................	9 7 0	,, Repairs to Building............................	25 0 9
,, Rent of Cottage, Hire of Lecture Room, &c.	15 0 0	,, Purchase of Periodicals & Newspapers, and for Printing,	44 2 8
		,, Librarian's Salary and Commission	14 7 11
		,, Donation to W. Traher	4 4 0
		,, Petty Expences, including Firing	11 15 5
			£212 6 9
		In Treasurer's hands..............	7 4 11½
	£219 11 8½		£219 11 8½

" We hereby certify that we have examined
" this Account of Receipts and Expences for
" the Year 1849, and that there is a Balance
" due to the Institution of £7. 4s. 11½d."

Signed,
J. GOLDEN,
J. BULLEN, } Auditors.

Highgate, 21st Feb. 1850.

THOMAS HILTON KEITH,
TREASURER.

The Ordinary member's subscription stood at one guinea (with smaller amounts for Associates) from 1839 until 1921, when it was raised to £1.5s. Further increases were small and infrequent until, starting in 1980, several large increases were made, taking subscriptions to £20 (Ordinary) and £30 (Household) at the end of the decade.

The table below indicates the fall in the 'real' value of the Ordinary subscription since 1839. Even the large increases in the 1980s brought its 1990 value to only three quarters of the original value. In the decade of the eighties however, the increase in the subscription outpaced inflation, so that the 'real' value of the subscription in 1990 was higher than it was in 1980.

SINGLE-MEMBER SUBSCRIPTION; YEARS OF CHANGE			
(omitting increases in 1956, '72', '76, '81, '85, '86)			
Decimal equivalent throughout			
	£	Value in 1839 terms Base £1.05	Value in 1980 terms Base £7.50
1839	1.05	1.05	
1921	1.25	0.70	
1938	1.50	1.23	
1949	2.00	1.14	
1980	7.50	0.51	7.50
1988	16.00	0.69	10.10
1989	20.00	0.80	11.68

Until 1980 it had been the policy of the Institution to hold down the subscription rates: unfortunately this did not encourage a growth in membership. One annual report after another carried appeals for more members, and for much of the Institution's history there have been financial worries.

For instance, the 1877 Report remarked that 'the trifling Annual Subscription of 21s. to the Institution is quite absorbed by current expenses'. And apart from a period in the mid–1980s there has seldom been a surplus to put to the repair fund.

The Institution's income has benefited increasingly from sources other than subscriptions: rents from 10A, the cottage in Swain's Lane and the garages, letting of the Lecture Hall and Reading Room, and a widening range of social activities. Yet the totals of income and expenditure looked small until the 1950s. The summary accounts in the 1849 Report, reproduced above, show the totals in balance at £220.

1849 was a good year for membership. In 1860 the accounts were balanced at £137, and as recently as 1947 the balance was at £990 income and expenditure. The corresponding figure for 1989 was £45,000. In 1990 a programme of measures to increase income was prepared so that the Institution could spend more in future years on salaried staff, repairs and decoration, furniture and equipment, and also create a fabric reserve fund.

Members have always been generous in their support of the Institution. As well as voluntary help of many sorts there have been numerous gifts and subscription lists to clear debts, many gifts of books, great efforts for fundraising activities, and contributions to appeals large and small.

On two occasions the appeals were to subscribe to formal loans. One was of £2,000 4% Loan Stock to finance the purchase of the freehold of 11 South Grove in 1932. The other, in 1936, was of a further £1,800 of the same Stock to purchase the Church House property. The Loan Stock was paid off in 1949–50.

In 1990 an appeal for a major Development Project raised some £240,000, mostly from members, and work started on extensive structural repairs and on the refurbishment of the Institution's building.

The educational purpose of the Institution has throughout its existence been of help financially. From its early years the Institution had exemption from local taxes under the Literary and Scientific Societies Act of 1843. Since the 1930s it has had charitable status, giving exemption from income tax and the benefit of the charity rebate on business rates assessed on its premises.

The Institution is an unincorporated society with trustees and since 1932 has been specially authorised under the Friendly Societies Acts.

CHAPTER FIVE

'Something for Curiosity, much for Pleasure, but more for Use'

The Library

The Institution has passed through several vicissitudes, but without doubt the main reason for its survival has been the Library. Situated on the edge of three London boroughs, none of which has ever provided a public library in or near the old village, the Institution fills the need. The central importance of the Library was recognised by John Henry Lloyd when for the celebration of the Institution's 50th Anniversary in 1889 he donated the proceeds of his *History and Antiquities of Highgate* for the purchase of 4,000 books. In the introduction to his book he says that he did so in the belief that 'the more valuable the Library, the more assured is the permanence of the Highgate Literary & Scientific Institution.'

At the end of its first year a collection of over 400 books had been acquired, which by 1845 had grown to nearly 2,000. In that year 12 periodicals were taken, including *The Quarterly Review, Edinburgh Review,* and *Foreign Quarterly Review,* and Charles Knight's *Penny Magazine.*

Rules for the inclusion of material in the Library were very strict: 'No book, pamphlet, publication or paper of any kind shall be introduced into the Institution...except by an order of the Committee; no such order shall be given unless with the written concurrence of two thirds of a Committee of at least six members, and one at least of the said members shall recommend the book, pamphlet or paper, from a knowledge of its character and tendency'.

When the Institution entered into what were to be its permanent premises in 1840, the Library was first housed in the room at the front of the building which is now the Reading Room.

The Librarian lived with his family in a flat on the first floor, and received a salary of 10 guineas a year. The care of the Institution premises, as well as attendance on borrowers and the sale of tickets for lectures were all part of his responsibilities. The Librarians for some years were not employed full time by the Institution, but had other jobs too. The first Librarian, Richard Whitmore, was in Customs and Excise, and a later holder of the office was an officer at Pentonville Gaol. Hours of opening of the Library were between 1 and 2pm (attended usually by his wife) and from 6 to 9pm in the evening. Wives and daughters frequently assisted with library duties and with the making of catalogues.

12. Catalogue of the first library of the Institution, March 1839. A small number of the original collection of books still remain in the Library – among them Gilbert White's Natural History of Selborne, *Russell's* History of Modern Europe *(4 vols. 1837), Richard Ford's* A Year in Spain *(1836), Clarke's* Life of Nelson *(1813), and* The Constitution of England *(1789).*

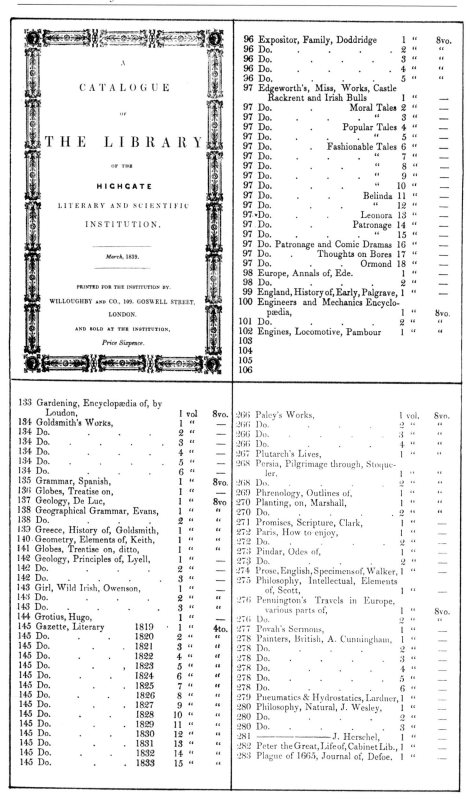

A

CATALOGUE

OF

THE LIBRARY

OF THE

HIGHGATE

LITERARY AND SCIENTIFIC

INSTITUTION.

March, 1839.

PRINTED FOR THE INSTITUTION BY.

WILLOUGHBY AND CO., 109. GOSWELL STREET,

LONDON.

AND SOLD AT THE INSTITUTION,

Price Sixpence.

96	Expositor, Family, Doddridge	1	"	8vo.
96	Do.	2	"	"
96	Do.	3	"	"
96	Do.	4	"	"
96	Do.	5	"	"
97	Edgeworth's, Miss, Works, Castle Rackrent and Irish Bulls	1	"	—
97	Do. Moral Tales	2	"	—
97	Do. "	3	"	—
97	Do. Popular Tales	4	"	—
97	Do. "	5	"	—
97	Do. Fashionable Tales	6	"	—
97	Do. "	7	"	—
97	Do. "	8	"	—
97	Do. "	9	"	—
97	Do. "	10	"	—
97	Do. Belinda	11	"	—
97	Do. "	12	"	—
97	Do. Leonora	13	"	—
97	Do. Patronage	14	"	—
97	Do. "	15	"	—
97	Do. Patronage and Comic Dramas	16	"	—
97	Do. Thoughts on Bores	17	"	—
97	Do. Ormond	18	"	—
98	Europe, Annals of, Ede.	1	"	—
98	Do.	2	"	—
99	England, History of, Early, Palgrave,	1	"	—
100	Engineers and Mechanics Encyclopædia,	1	"	8vo.
101	Do.	2	"	"
102	Engines, Locomotive, Pambour	1	"	"
103				
104				
105				
106				

133	Gardening, Encyclopædia of, by Loudon,	1 vol.		8vo.
134	Goldsmith's Works,	1	"	—
134	Do.	2	"	—
134	Do.	3	"	—
134	Do.	4	"	—
134	Do.	5	"	—
134	Do.	6	"	—
135	Grammar, Spanish,	1	"	8vo.
136	Globes, Treatise on,	1	"	—
137	Geology, De Luc,	1	"	8vo
138	Geographical Grammar, Evans,	1	"	"
138	Do.	2	"	"
139	Greece, History of, Goldsmith,	1	"	"
140	Geometry, Elements of, Keith,	1	"	"
141	Globes, Treatise on, ditto,	1	"	"
142	Geology, Principles of, Lyell,	1	"	—
142	Do.	2	"	—
142	Do.	3	"	—
143	Girl, Wild Irish, Owenson,	1	"	—
143	Do.	2	"	"
143	Do.	3	"	"
144	Grotius, Hugo,	1	"	—
145	Gazette, Literary 1819	1	"	4to.
145	Do. 1820	2	"	"
145	Do. 1821	3	"	"
145	Do. 1822	4	"	"
145	Do. , 1823	5	"	"
145	Do. 1824	6	"	"
145	Do. 1825	7	"	"
145	Do. 1826	8	"	"
145	Do. 1827	9	"	"
145	Do. 1828	10	"	"
145	Do. 1829	11	"	"
145	Do. 1830	12	"	"
145	Do. 1831	13	"	"
145	Do. 1832	14	"	"
145	Do. 1833	15	"	"

266	Paley's Works,	1 vol.		8vo.
266	Do.	2	"	"
266	Do.	3	"	"
266	Do.	4	"	"
267	Plutarch's Lives,	1	"	"
268	Persia, Pilgrimage through, Stoqueler.	1	"	"
268	Do.	2	"	"
269	Phrenology, Outlines of,	1	"	"
270	Planting, on, Marshall,	1	"	"
270	Do.	2	"	"
271	Promises, Scripture, Clark,	1	"	—
272	Paris, How to enjoy,	1	"	—
272	Do.	2	"	—
273	Pindar, Odes of,	1	"	—
273	Do.	2	"	—
274	Prose, English, Specimens of, Walker,	1	"	—
275	Philosophy, Intellectual, Elements of, Scott,	1	"	—
276	Pennington's Travels in Europe, various parts of,	1	"	8vo.
276	Do.	2	"	"
277	Povah's Sermons,	1	"	—
278	Painters, British, A. Cunningham,	1	"	—
278	Do.	2	"	—
278	Do.	3	"	—
278	Do.	4	"	—
278	Do.	5	"	—
278	Do.	6	"	—
279	Pneumatics & Hydrostatics, Lardner,	1	"	—
280	Philosophy, Natural, J. Wesley,	1	"	—
280	Do.	2	"	—
280	Do.	3	"	—
281	——————J. Herschel,	1	"	—
282	Peter the Great, Life of, Cabinet Lib.,	1	"	—
283	Plague of 1665, Journal of, Defoe.	1	"	—

*13. The Institution
Library 1902, with Mr
and Mrs Henry Holt,
the Librarians. The
clock is American,
1876, and is still in
the Library.*

Acquisition of stock for the Library depended greatly on donations from members. To supplement these with more up-to-date works, a subscription to Mudie's Library was taken out in 1860, which brought a changing selection of 40 volumes. By 1873 this was no longer satisfactory; it was becoming difficult to obtain the books which were wanted, so the subscription was cut, the money saved being spent on buying books. The scheme of loans from a commercial library was tried again in 1937, when a subscription of £25 per annum was taken out with Harrods Library. This worked very well for quite a few years, but as the number of books borrowed was related to the price, e.g. a book valued up to £1 was counted as one book, up to 30s. as two books, up to £2 as four books, etc. by the mid–1960s the subscription had ceased to be economic and it was discontinued in 1967.

By the mid–1860s there seems to have been a decline in reading standards – the Annual Reports complain that 'a preponderance of issues of Periodicals, and the works which issue from Mudie's Library, is only in accordance with the spirit of the age, and with that taste for light literature which so generally prevails', and regret the failure to take out standard works of science and literature. The books in the library appear also to have been getting in a poor state of repair, and appeals were issued for good copies of the better books.

After the great rebuilding of the premises in 1880, the Library moved to its present location in the large high room at the back of the building. The walls were covered with shelving, with fixed shelves which by the 1980s, with the larger size of hard-backed books, have become inconvenient and cramped.

The Institution was by the 1880s one of the few such still existing. The new developments, and the feeling of renewed life which they brought, led to an immense increase in membership, to a total of 600. The previous maximum had been 400.

This progress continued for some years. In 1890 there was a record membership of 702 and the number of books borrowed in 1892 was nearly 14,000. There is an interesting sidelight on the tastes of the reading public in the Annual Report for that year. Speaking of the importance of attaining the habit of reading, the Report goes on 'there is real pleasure in reading a good novel – the misfortune is that they are comparatively few'. Further on we read: 'There is no three-volume trash on our shelves.'

The climate of seriousness in which the Institution movement began was changing, and the high moral tone was not so easy to maintain in the face of competition from the Public Libraries. Membership declined during the first part of the 20th century, with an improvement in the Thirties, when money for buying books was raised by the holding of Whist Drives.

There was a growing interest in the collection of material relating to the district. The 1934 Annual Report reads: 'In these days of constant change and alteration of the neighbourhood by modernisation and rebuilding, the importance of such a repository of material relating to the appearance and history of Old Highgate Village should appeal to all residents (new or old) who have the interests of the neighbourhood at heart.' This realisation of the necessity for preserving the evidence of the past increased greatly and led to the creation in 1974 of the Institution's Archives Committee.

In 1939 the Institution celebrated its centenary, and at this time both the Reading Room and the Library were entirely renovated. Up to this time the walls had been covered with framed prints and paintings: these were taken down, many were removed from their frames for storage in portfolios, while a more modest selection was re-hung; and new comfortable armchairs replaced the old bentwood chairs in the Reading Room to create the impression of a pleasant sitting room. In 1978 the Institution was given an old grate with a cast-iron fireback, dated 1632, with the coat-of-arms of King Charles I; it was decided that the fireplace in the Reading Room should be opened up to take this, and when the 1930s surround was removed the original 18th-century fireplace and chimney breast were exposed.

With the onset of the Second World War, problems were caused by falling membership owing to service in the Forces and evacuation. In 1944 a flying bomb fell in Waterlow Park, causing considerable damage even in South Grove. The Institution and the Congregational Church along the way were among the buildings to suffer. First aid repairs were done at this time, and a temporary library was set up in the Committee Room and passage. Later, when the major war damage repairs were carried out in 1948, a temporary library was established for some months by transferring the standing book stacks into the Lecture Hall.

After the war there was a major clearance of books. It was felt that with the advances in science which had taken place in the last fifty years, our collections in that area had become out-dated, and many old standard works were given to various scientific libraries. There had been a previous clearance in 1937, when many 19th-century works were disposed of. The lists of these books still exist: the cost to replace them today would be enormous, but at the time it was difficult even to give them away.

By the 1960s the Library numbered some 30,000 volumes. A small book fund allowed for the purchase of a reasonable number of new books; in addition the Edith Ellen Harris Trust presented a selection of good non-fiction books from time to time, A group of 'Friends of the Library' was started, the members of which gave one book each year.

Over the years the Library has gained from donations of books, including the Talbot Baines Reed collection of children's books given in memory of the writer of boys' stories. In 1968 a sum of money was raised to buy books in memory of Elaine Vaughan who had been Librarian of the Institution for 29 years.

By the early 1970s the Institution was beginning to spend considerable sums on books, sums stretched by buying from library suppliers who gave discounts. The present sum made available from Institution funds for the purchase of books is just over £2,000 a year.

Since the 1960s the membership of the Institution has more than doubled and the make-up has changed. Whereas before the Second World War the population of Highgate was fairly static, in the years after the War population movement increased considerably, and a much greater number of younger people with children made their appearance. To cater for this the number of books in the children's section has been greatly increased and its location changed to be nearer the entrance.

14. The Institution Reading Room before its complete refurbishment for the centenary celebrations in 1939. At that time many of the pictures were removed, and the bentwood chairs were replaced with comfortable armchairs.

With the advent of television and the wide availability and cheapness of paperbacks, people's reading habits have changed. Where previously they carried away an armful of books they now take fewer and over the years the proportion of non-fiction books has risen.

Much more has been done in recent years to interest the membership in the Library's activities. In 1984 the first of a continuing series of most successful Literary Dinners took place. Annual Book Sales, which raise on average £1,000 each time, are among events intended to raise funds to help the Institution; for these, members give books for sale – the Library benefits from these gifts by keeping some for its own stock.

The Librarian is a key figure in the running of the Institution as a whole. The Institution has been most fortunate in the people who, assisted in several cases by their families, have held this position, and Annual Reports have paid tribute to their 'excellence and devotion'. Only in one year were the tenures of office short: in 1860 Mr Noakes died after a few months. The son, C. Noakes found 'the duties incompatible with his private engagements'. He was succeeded by Charles Lee, and the 22nd Report said 'the office of Librarian has once more been filled (it is hoped, under Providence, for years to come).' Providence smiled and Librarians stayed for a considerable number of years, notably Charles Lee (1861–75), Charles B. Scott (1878–82), James Drummond (1882–95), Henry Holt (1895–1903), who was assisted by his wife and two daughters, and Alfred Holmes (1903–29), who came from the Geological Society and 'together with his wife and daughter entered into the life of the Institution with enthusiasm and gave the greatest satisfaction to all subscribers'.

Among the longest serving of all have been our two latest Librarians – Elaine Vaughan (1939–68) and her daughter Gwynydd Gosling, who retired this year after 22 years. When Elaine Vaughan took office the Institution had just been celebrating its centenary and was planning an extension and improvement of its premises. These plans had to be shelved at the outbreak of War in 1939 and instead – in the words of Sir James Brown – 'The Institution was faced with a battle even to survive. Mrs Vaughan set herself to the task of keeping the Institution and Library open and at the service of members; much of the anxiety and responsibility during the period of the air-raids fell upon her, with the assistance after 1941 of Miss Pyemont. They kept the flag flying throughout the whole of the War and the Library open and in valued use despite war damage to the building. The Institution's record of unbroken history, of which we are all justly proud, is thus due to the devoted work of its Librarians during those difficult days.'

Elaine Vaughan also played an important role in the social activities of the Institution and in paying tribute to her personal qualities Sir James Brown wrote: 'Many found in her a most sympathetic listener to confidences when the business was merely the routine exchange of a book'.

Gwynydd carried on her mother's work. Librarianship is in her family's tradition since her grandfather, Edward Wood, was a librarian from 1895 to 1942, and they both received the Silver Jubilee Medal, her grandfather in 1935 and she herself in 1977, for their services as Librarians. As well as fulfilling her duties as Librarian Gwynydd Gosling will be particularly remembered for her work on the Institution's archives, and as being the inspiration and organiser behind its Exhibitions. She has preserved the Library as a focal point in the Village – in her own words 'We know everyone by name and we know the books they want to read. We know about their lives because it's the sort of place people come to when they want to talk. There is a good feeling here and it's a feeling we're careful to preserve.'

The Library could not operate without its loyal band of voluntary helpers, who since 1985 have taken charge of the counter for a morning or an afternoon a week; they relieve the Librarian and her assistant Mrs Butler for work such as the purchase and cataloguing of books, and the routine office work. Contact with the members is a most important part of the Librarian's duties, to enable their needs to be catered for. An increasing part of this work is dealing with school children seeking books for school projects, and also local authors needing research material. One member of the Library Committee is responsible for dealing with books which are overdue. The first mention of this problem appears in the Annual Report for 1863, so human nature has changed little.

The physical appearance of the Library has changed considerably since the 1960s. The old anthracite stove was removed and replaced by the Library counter, more standing book stacks have been added and modern ladders have replaced the old ladder-on-wheels, up which children loved to climb.

15. *The Institution Library in 1958. The Library was renovated a few years after this, when the anthracite stove on the left was removed and replaced by a counter. The tall ladder on wheels on the right, beloved by generations of children who rode on it, also disappeared at this time.*

16. *The Fox and Crown, Highgate West Hill. The courtyard of this old pub is still evident attached to the house at No. 40. The place relished its notoriety after the landlord saved the young Queen Victoria from serious injury in 1837, when he arrested her runaway coach on the steep hill. An enormous coat-of-arms (a reward for his services) is displayed on the building, and the chair in which the queen recovered from the experience is placed in a prominent position by the front door. The building was demolished in 1895 and the coat-of-arms rehoused in the Institution.*

Some relics of the old days remain in the Library: the magnificent coat-of-arms given by Queen Victoria to the innkeeper of the Fox and Crown who stopped her runaway coach on Highgate West Hill in 1837, just after her accession; the late–19th-century double-faced clock which shows, besides the time, the day, date and month, and the pair of ram's horns formerly used in the old ceremony of 'Swearing on the Horns' at a public house (now disappeared) in the High Street called The Cooper's Arms. This custom, dating from the days of the drovers, is still carried on at different public houses in the Village, for charity.

As mentioned at the beginning of this chapter, there is no public library in the immediate neighbourhood, and the nearest branch libraries of Haringey and Camden, as a consequence of the recent cuts, are both open for fewer hours than the Institution. As long ago as 1887 the Annual Report had commented: 'The Institution possesses the only public library in Highgate, and indeed in the whole Parish'. 'The rising generation is a reading generation, and with the spread of higher education will become more so, and mental food must be provided for them. Books are now a necessity, and libraries are the storehouses of literature, from whence we may gather something for curiosity, much for pleasure, but more for use; and in what shape can books possibly be made more accessible than by the co-operation offered by an institution of this character? In forming a good library we are spreading the light of knowledge, insensibly influencing the future, not only of Highgate, but also of England: for as our old village has been associated with some noble names in the past, why should Highgate, with greater opportunities, be less distinguished in the future?'

An ambitious claim, and yet, as Lord Brougham, the pioneer of the Institution movement had earlier said: 'Knowledge is power', and where better to gain such knowledge than in a good library, even in these days of television and computers?

CHAPTER SIX

'Time present and time past
Are both perhaps present in time future
And time future contained in time past'
T.S. Eliot.

The Archives

THE ARCHIVE ROOM

The Institution has always been a depository for all kinds of archive material relating not only to the Institution itself, its history and activities, but also to other organisations and societies in Highgate and neighbouring areas as well as to distinguished local residents. Some of the material has been donated, some bequeathed and some specifically collected by members of the Institution, notably by J.H. Lloyd, George Potter and Sir James Brown. All three were great collectors of local history material and were much concerned with building up, and organising, the rich collection of source material being accumulated in the archives.

For years most of this material was inadequately stored in brown paper parcels in cupboards and under the stage in the Lecture Hall. In 1974, at the suggestion of Dame Geraldine Aves (a prominent member of the Institution and Chairman of the Library Committee), a small working party was set up 'to record, display and store the archives'. This became a sub-committee of the Library Committee and in 1977 a fully independent Committee, which meets weekly to sort and catalogue existing acquisitions and to organise new material. In 1983, through the generosity of local benefactors, the Institution's cellars were renovated to provide a room with controlled humidity and storage space. The specially designed cupboards and cabinets house documents, records, letters, portraits, prints and photographs, all indexed and accessible to researchers and anyone interested in the history of the Institution or of Highgate. The collections are widely known both at home and abroad, and well used.

In addition to caring for the archives the Committee is responsible for organising exhibitions.

THE COLLECTION

The Highgate Collection, as it might well be called, contains much unusual, sometimes unique, material. For example, original documents relating to the founding of the Institution itself are held, together with extensive records of its later development. It contains interesting correspondence, much

of it handwritten, between the officers of the Institution and potential lecturers, including such celebrated figures as Matthew Arnold, A.E. Housman and J.B. Priestley. The photographic collection includes two bequests: one of glass negatives taken mostly in the 1880s by a professional photographer called Sulman, and the second of photographs of Highgate taken by Sir James Brown during the years 1940 to 1965. There are also a number of photographs of local landmarks in Highgate Village and the surrounding areas (Cromwell House, Kenwood, the Burdett-Coutts estate etc.) and of celebrated local personalities.

Two individual collections are of particular importance – the Coleridge Collection and the Betjeman Collection.

THE COLERIDGE COLLECTION

From 1816 until his death in 1834, Samuel Taylor Coleridge lived in Highgate with a local physician, Dr James Gillman, and his family, at first in Moreton House in South Grove and subsequently at No. 3 The Grove. On his death he was buried in the grounds of Highgate Old Chapel, but in 1961 his remains were transferred to St Michael's Church in South Grove. Many of his most important works were published during his years in Highgate, including *Kubla Khan*, *Biographia Literaria* and most of his philosophical and theological works.

The collection includes an oil portrait of Coleridge painted by Madame de Predl at Dr Gillman's house; two letters from Coleridge to John Smith of Sheffield and to Lancelot Wade of Bristol; copies of his published works,

17. Samuel Taylor Coleridge, by Mme de Predl. Portrait in oils of the poet who lived in Highgate from 1816 until his death in 1834.

18. Sir John Betjeman, Poet Laureate, born in Parliament Hill Mansions in 1906; his family moved to 31 Highgate West Hill in 1907, where they remained until c1918. A photograph from the Institution's Betjeman Collection.

together with a good collection of biographical and critical material; photographs, prints, and extensive research material.

THE BETJEMAN COLLECTION
As a child Sir John Betjeman lived in Highgate West Hill and was a pupil first at Byron House and later at Highgate Junior School. Although he never again lived in Highgate after leaving school, he retained vivid memories of his childhood and in 1960 he wrote the Introduction to the catalogue of an Institution Exhibition on Highgate celebrities, in which he referred affectionately to Highgate as it was when he was a boy. The collection (supported from the beginning by the Betjeman family and his principal publisher, John Murray) includes an original draft of a Betjeman poem (in manuscript) later expanded into the poem *Cornish Cliffs*; numerous signed letters, some of them in manuscript; copies of his published work, including valuable first editions, some of which are signed by the author; newspaper cuttings, reviews, drawings, photographs and memorabilia of all kinds. It is a living collection constantly being updated and has benefited from some generous donations: it was started with the gift of a whole collection of first editions.

LOCAL ORGANISATIONS
The archives also contain papers deposited with the Institution for safe-keeping by local organisations or societies. These include:

The Highgate Book Society
Founded in 1822, the first subscribers included Dr Gillman, the friend and patron of Coleridge,. The Society continued until 1922, at which time its records were deposited with the Institution.

The Mothercraft Training Society
In 1918 Sir Frederic Truby King, an obstetrician who had greatly reduced the infant mortality rate in New Zealand, was invited to set up and chair the Mothercraft Training Society in London. From 1925 onwards the Society was based in Cromwell House, and when it was finally disbanded in 1951, its records were deposited with the Institution. These include books for the guidance of mothers on how to care for their babies (some by King), magazines and reports of the Society, photographs, lecture notes and other miscellaneous material.

The Wollaston and Pauncefort Almshouses
The Almshouses in Southwood Lane in Highgate were founded in 1656 by Sir John Wollaston, the owner of Hornsey manor, and are still in existence. The documents include the Deeds of the original Almshouses, accounts, Minutes and lists of residents from 1730–1880, applications for admittance 1902–22 and a table of regulations.

The Highgate Horticultural Society and **Robert Whipple Trust**
The Institution houses the records of the Horticultural Society (one of the

oldest societies in Highgate, having been founded in 1859) and the Robert Whipple Trust (founded in 1952) which among its activities sponsors an annual Institution lecture.

EXHIBITIONS

In the early years there were few, if any, exhibitions mounted by the Institution. There is a reference in an early Minute, dated 3 June 1843, to a floral exhibition to take place between 2 June and 1 July, but whether it did or not remains unverified. An exhibition of roses was, however, held in the summer of 1845 in the garden of the then President of the Institution, Harry Chester; and in October 1893 the Highgate Artists held their first exhibition at the Institution; this subsequently became a biennial event until October 1913.

The first recorded exhibition mounted by the Institution itself, on War Trophies, was held in 1917 under the direction of the then President, D. Croal Thompson. This was visited by hundreds of people, and the substantial sum raised was donated to the hospital set up in Highgate during the War.

Although in the early years many exhibitions were organised by local groups, and occasionally by individuals, it was not until the 1950s that the Institution began regularly to arrange its own. The Institution mounted an exhibition of handicrafts, the work of members and local residents, and another exhibition entitled *Europe in Highgate* – pictures, books and examples of European arts and crafts collected by the members.

The Institution's archives have been a rich inspiration for exhibitions since 1963, when *Pictures of Old Highgate* was so popular in the spring that it was

19. The first Exhibition displaying the Institution's Archives, February 1977.

20. 'The Heart of a London Village'. *The latest Exhibition, to celebrate the Institution's 150th anniversary, taken entirely from the Institution's collection, May 1989.*

repeated in the autumn. Since then *Chapters of Village History* (1966–67 for Haringey Arts Festival) has been followed by, among others, *London at our Feet* (1967), *The 130th Birthday of the Institution* (1969), *The Northern Heights of London* (1970) and *The Institution, its History and Personalities* (1980).

Highgate and its personalities have often been the inspiration for exhibitions. In March 1960 *Some Highgate Celebrities* displayed portraits and photographs of well-known residents of Highgate from the 16th century onwards including Andrew Marvell, the Marquis of Dorchester, Baroness Burdett-Coutts, Charles Green the balloonist and Samuel Taylor Coleridge. The following year *Highgate Today* highlighted the work of Henry Jackson, probably the last master craftsman in the Village, who finally retired from business in the late 1960s.

Coleridge has been a subject for exhibitions since 1972 when the noted Coleridge authority, Professor Kathleen Coburn, opened a celebration of the bi-centenary of the poet's birth. It attracted over 1,100 visitors. In 1983 *Coleridge and Highgate* was part of a Coleridge Week marking the 150th anniversary of the consecration of St Michael's Church. It showed what life was like in Highgate during his lifetime. The catalogue had an introduction by the Institution's own Coleridge scholar, the Librarian, Gwynydd Gosling, who did the same for an exhibition the following year. *Coleridge and his World* was opened by Dr John Beer of Peterhouse, Cambridge: there followed a week celebrating the poet which included lectures on *Coleridge the Man* and *Coleridge's Battle with Drug Addiction*, and an evening of *Readings from Coleridge*.

In 1986 it was the turn of John Betjeman. *Summoned by Bells – Betjeman Remembered* celebrated the man, the poet, his life and links with Highgate. It owed much to the interest of Highgate bookseller, Antony Wilson, who persuaded the poet's daughter, Candida Lycett-Green, to loan some of the family treasures. In the exhibition were paintings, portraits and photographs of Betjeman and his friends and contemporaries, photographs of churches he wrote about as well as his boater, autographed letters and copies of published works, some signed by the author.

The Archives Committee contributed to the celebrations for the Institution's 150th birthday in 1989 by mounting an exhibition of material drawn exclusively from its own resources. This would not have been possible but for the assiduous work on the Institution's archives which had been going on for close on two decades. *The Heart of a London Village* highlighted the different activities of the Institution since its foundation. The week-long exhibition attracted over 600 visitors.

CHAPTER SEVEN

'To stimulate and gratify an intelligent desire for information'

Lectures and Activities

An outstanding feature of the Institution's activities is the Tuesday lecture which takes place every week from September to May. Philip Howard has paid tribute to the survival of 'that almost forgotten Victorian art form the public lecture.' He goes on to say 'It [Highgate] is no mean village. Many Highgate villagers are well-connected bossy intellectuals, which is how, year in year out, they persuade eminent celebs to come and talk to them for free. It is impossible to say no to such earnest good nature still on that unfashionable Victorian hunt for sweetness and light. The lovingly preserved records of lecturers going back 150 years form a roll-call of the British intelligentsia, academics and men and women of culture: the true apostles of equality.'

THE LECTURE PROGRAMME
The Tuesday lecture programme started at the Gate House within a few weeks of the Institution's foundation in January 1839. The initial quartet of lectures – The Atmosphere; Water; Heat; Light and Electricity was followed by two short series: one on Geography and Geology, and the other on Botany. In the early months of 1840, still at the Gate House, another series followed on Zoology, Astronomy and Man, 'the whole intended to excite an interest in Nature, animate and inanimate; and to display throughout the whole, the power, wisdom and goodness of the great Lawgiver'.

Among the first lectures to be given when the Institution moved into new premises later in 1840 were three on the 'Empire of Russia' by the Institution's Hon. Secretary, the Rev. Richard Carter Smith. These accounts, worthy fore-runners of many interesting lectures to come on travel and exploration, were illustrated by models and exhibits based on the speaker's personal travels and adventures. During the next few decades scientific lectures predominated, frequently reflecting the momentous discoveries, inventions and preoccupations of the age.

The following are examples:

1843
Aerostration – 'The science of raising, suspending and guiding machines in the air'.
Lecturer: T. Nutter.
(The first successful ascent by a powered balloon was in 1852.)

1857
Principles and practical details of the proposed Atlantic Telegraph.
Lecturer: T. Allen.
(The first landlines were laid in 1844. The Atlantic telegraph was begun in 1857 and completed in 1865.)

1861
The total eclipse of the sun as seen in Spain by the Expedition sent out for that purpose.
Lecturer: F.W. Burr.
(There had been an eclipse in 1860.)

1870
The Channel Railway.
Lecturer: William T. Walker.
(There had been proposals, supported by geological investigations and borings, for a Channel Tunnel in 1856 and 1868.)

1879
The Telephone and the Microphone.
Lecturer: A.B. Harding.
(The telephone was invented in 1876 by Bell, and the microphone by Hughes in 1878.)

1880
Possibilities of Aerial Navigation.
Lecturer: F.W. Breary.
(The first ascent of Zeppelin was in 1900, and of the Wright Bros. in 1903.)

1880
Recent discoveries in Radiant Matter.
Lecturer: A. B. Harding.
(Discoveries of Cathode Rays 1859, X-Rays 1895 and Radio-activity in 1896.)

1881
The Electric Light (with brilliant experiments).
Lecturer: A.B. Harding.

1883
The Electric Light in our Homes.
Lecturer: R. Hammond (Man. Dir. of Hammond Electric Light Co.).
(The first practical electric light was devised independently by T.A. Edison and J.W. Swan in 1880.)

1878
The facts of Natural History, compared with the 'Hypothesis of Darwinism'.
Lecturer: W. Hawkins.

1882
Charles Darwin.
Lecturer: The Hon. Mr Justice Fry, President H.L.S.I.

1891
Evolution: its meaning and value.
Lecturer: E.A. Parkyn (University of Cambridge).
(Darwin's *On the Origin of species by means of Natural Selection* was published in 1859.)

1887
Faraday
Lecturer: Professor Charles Tomlinson, FRS, Vice-President H.L.S.I.
(Faraday's Law of Electrolysis was published in 1834. He died in 1867.)

21. Fanny Kemble (Mrs Butler), actress, daughter of Charles Kemble, niece of Sarah Siddons, gave her first public readings from Shakespeare at the Institution in 1848.

1896
X-Rays
Lecturer: H.C. Harrison.
(X-Rays were discovered by Röntgen in 1895.)

1896
The Electric Telegraph (with limelight illustrations)
Lecturer: William Lynd.

1898
Telegraphy without wires (illustrated with experiments and with lantern slides).
Lecturer: R. Kerr.
(Radio-Telegraphy was invented by Marconi in 1895. He conducted transmission experiments across the Bristol Channel in 1897, and across the English Channel in 1899.)

22. Mary Kingsley (1863–1900), niece of the Rev. Charles Kingsley, lived for the first 17 years of her life in Southwood Lane. She lectured twice at the Institution about her travels in West Africa and wrote Travels in West Africa *and* West African Studies'.

It is easy to picture the interest aroused in Highgate by these 19th-century lectures. Packed audiences assembled on the Tuesday evenings. Even those who did not attend could sometimes reap the benefit thanks to meticulous coverage in the *Hampstead and Highgate Express* in the following week.

The twentieth century ushered in other scientific subjects; the following are examples: Submarine Telegraphy (1925), Television and Noctovision

(1930 and 1935), Large Telescopes (1937, given by the Astronomer Royal), Telecommunication (1981), Computers in the Home (1982 and 1985), The Thames Barrier (1983) and Nuclear Magnetic Resonance (1987). These lectures show that the Institution remains a place for intelligent laymen to learn about innovations and advances in science and technology.

This emphasis on science should not detract from the value of the literary lectures which have been a mainstay of the programme from the earliest days. Something of the richness, variety and fascination of these lectures may perhaps be gained by dividing them into groups and highlighting some of the themes.

LITERATURE AND THE ARTS

1854
Photography.
Lecturer: Roger Fenton, founder and first secretary of the Photographic Society.

1857
Samuel Richardson – His Life and Times.
Lecturer: A. Birrell.

1870
Dante and Italian Literature.
Lecturer: Leone Levi.

23. Dame Millicent Garrett Fawcett (1847–1930), social reformer, author and President of the National Union of Women's Suffrage Society. During the series of lectures to mark the Institution's 50th year in 1889, she spoke on The Social Position of Women: its progress during the last 100 years.

24. Sophie Bryant (1850–1922), one of the first women to gain a degree at London University. In 1880 she gave a series of ten lectures on Moral Ideals, Ancient & Modern *at the HLSI*

25. Mrs Faith Cope Morgan, member of the Institution, who, on 26 November 1929, gave a lecture Across Africa by Motor Lorry. *The text of the lecture is in the Institution's collection.*

26. Arthur Waley (1889–1966), world-renowned translator of Chinese and Japanese poetry. He gave a reading of his translations of Chinese poetry at the Institution in 1964. He is buried in Highgate Cemetery. This photograph, by Alison Waley, was taken in his garden in Southwood Lane in 1963 on the day of the car crash which paralysed him.

1873
Coleridge.
Lecturer: John Sime, President of H.L.S.I.

1882
The Language and Literature of China.
Lecturer: R.K. Douglas, Professor of Chinese at King's College.

1886
Robert Browning: Poet and Prophet.
Lecturer: Rev. J.S. Jones.

1886
William Wordsworth.
Lecturer: J.T. Maude.

1888
The Poetry of the Reign (during celebrations of the Institution's Golden Jubilee).
Lecturer: Sir Edmund Gosse.

1888
A General View of Victorian Literature.
Lecturer: Professor John W. Hales.

1894
A Thousand years of Dictionary Making.
Lecturer: Sir J.A. H. Murray.

1964
Readings of Chinese Poetry.
Lecturer: Arthur Waley.

1987
What Men or Gods are these? A Mythological Tour of the National Gallery.
Lecturer: Isabel Raphael.

1989
Samuel Taylor Coleridge.
Lecturer: Richard Holmes.

TRAVEL AND EXPLORATION

1869
Personal Experiences in Egypt and Turkey.
Lecturer: Sir Sydney Waterlow.

1897
Tales of a Tropical Traveller.

1899
Experiences in West Africa.
Lecturer: Mary Kingsley.

1904
The Great Siberian Railway.
Lecturer: A. Montefiore Brice FRGS.

1929
Across Africa by Motor-Lorry.
Lecturer: Faith Cope-Morgan.

1958
Antarctica.
Lecturer: David Stratton, Dep. Leader British Trans-Antarctica Expedition 1957–58.

HISTORICAL AND SOCIOLOGICAL

1887
The Social Position of Women: its progress during the last 100 years.
Lecturer: Millicent Garrett Fawcett, Leader of the Women's Suffrage Movement.

1891
Count Tolstoi: Novelist and Social Reformer.
Lecturer: Sergius Stepniak – Pseudonym of Sergey Mikhaylovich Kravinchsky, writer on conditions and revolutionary movements in Russia.

1892
Caen Wood and its Associations.
Lecturer: John Henry Lloyd.

1917
Nationalities.
Lecturer: Dr Sophie Bryant.

1977
Co-existing with the Soviet Union.
Lecturer: Lord Brimelow.

In the 1988–89 season – as part of the Institution's 150th anniversary celebrations – the programme offered a series of lectures linked with those given in the early days of the Institution, illustrating perhaps more of a continuity of interest over the ages than one might have imagined. Examples are: *Artistic Taste in the 1830s and 1840s* (Brian Cairns, 1989); *Darwin's Voyage of the Beagle* (Dr Wilma George, 1989); *Fox Talbot and the early days of Photography* (John Ward, 1989); *Michael Faraday: His Home and Work* (Sir George Porter, 1989).

The Institution has been fortunate in receiving endowments for three series of lectures. The Whipple Trust was set up 'for the advancement of education and learning in any part of England and more particularly in the Village of Highgate'. The first Whipple Trust Lecture was given in 1953, and among notable lectures have been *Turning points in the History of Medicine* by Lord Taylor of Harlow, *Georgian Poets* by Christopher Hassall, *The Size of the Galaxy* by Richard van der Tiet Woolley, the Astronomer Royal, *The Stuart Age – its place in our history* by C.V. Wedgwood, *Can Gorbachev succeed?* by Sir Bryan Cartledge, H.M. Ambassador to Moscow 1985–88.

Dr Mahomed Aslam endowed an annual lecture in memory of his wife Dr Hilda Aslam, née Hulme, a lecturer at London University and a specialist in the language of Shakespeare. The Hilda Aslam lecturers have included a number of well-known speakers: Sir Huw Weldon on *Image and Reputation: reflections on communication*, Julia Neuberger on *Harps, Hymns and Hittites: the influence of the Biblical David on English Literature*, Richard Holmes on *Coleridge – Early Visions* and Michael Foot on *Hampstead Heath: a second cradle for the Romantics*.

Kathleen Budgett-Meakin, a former Secretary of the Institution and whose husband, Denzil, had formerly been a Trustee, has provided the third fund: the first lecture was given in 1990 on *The Secret Founts of Love: Dante's In Vita Nuova*, by William Anderson.

Certain activities quite separate from the lectures were known as *conversaziones* and *soirées*. A typical *conversazione* was that of April 1885, given to close the season. On display were 'a working model of an electric locomotive' and 'a type of writing machine', microscopes, water colours and drawings; recitals from Shakespeare, Dickens and Sheridan were given by the Misses Webling, and a violin solo by G.H. Betjemann of the Royal Italian Opera, Covent Garden.

From 1895 until the First World War the opening event of the season was a reception given by 'the President and his lady'. These functions continued between the Wars, but after the Second World War were not resumed until 1954. For some years there were 'social evenings' to mark the opening and closing of a season; more recently social functions have been associated with particular events, such as the opening of exhibitions, following the Hilda Aslam lecture, and the President's 150th Anniversary Reception in January 1989. Since 1980 a 'New Members' party has been held in January of each year.

CHRISTMAS ENTERTAINMENT

Christmas entertainment has been a long-standing feature of the Institution's programme of social activities and its character has changed over the years. In the early days it was very much for children. The first entertainment in 1845 involved a magic lantern hired at £1.10s. for the night. For the next ninety years or so the entertainment, for both young and old, consisted of legerdemain, clowns, dissolving views, a 'polyphonist', magic, ventriloquists, conjurers, marionettes, jugglers or shadowgraphy. World War Two temporarily suspended jollifications, but in December 1951 the 'Christmas Party' made its appearance, an adult function, which continues to the present time.

The Institution's 100th birthday was celebrated by a dinner and dance at the Criterion Restaurant in Piccadilly Circus in January 1939. October 1980, the centenary of the opening of the Lecture Hall, was made another social occasion.

From 1960 until 1974 the Highgate Dance, organised by Isla Merry, was held regularly in January, originally in the dining hall of Highgate School and later in the Institution. In May 1989 a Masked Ball was held jointly with the Highgate Society at Channing School as part of the Institution's 150th anniversary celebration.

Whist drives were popular in the 1920s and 30s, but during the 1960s bridge became more popular. Since 1969 there have been informal bridge-playing sessions, organised by Ruth Emms on two afternoons a week.

During the nineteenth century music played an important role and the first known concert was given at the Institution in April 1843. An outstanding series of five chamber music concerts were conducted by G.H. Betjemann of the Royal Italian Opera, Covent Garden in 1884, 1885 and 1886 and aroused great interest in musical circles outside Highgate, receiving favourable notices in the *Morning Post*. During the twentieth century there was a gradual decline in the popularity of dramatic and musical recitals.

EDUCATIONAL

Educational activities first occur in the Minutes of 1 December 1841, where reference is made to an Instrumental Musical Class 'in progress'. Before long there were classes in Vocal Music, French and Drawing, and from 1857 additional classes in English, History, Composition, Grammar, Butler's *Analogy of Religion*, Euclid and Algebra – all given without payment by members of the Institution. This flurry of enthusiasm was perhaps misjudged. The following year's Annual Report indicated that the only two classes still being held were Singing on the Sol-fa system, and Arithmetic and Elementary Maths.

During the Crimean War the Institution set up classes in Reading, Writing and Arithmetic for soldiers of the militia stationed in Highgate. The classes were for six months from 10 October 1855 with a paid teacher, plus the assistance of 'such gentlemen as may be disposed to give gratuitous tuition'. At a meeting in March 1856 prizes were given for regular attendance and the winners were recommended for promotion.

In 1870 a circular was sent out announcing 'Educational Lectures for

27. Eleanor Marx (1855–1898), daughter of Karl Marx. She too is buried in Highgate Cemetery.

28. Leaflet for a Class for the Study of Shakespeare's As You Like It, *which it was proposed that Eleanor Marx should direct at the Institution in 1884.*

Ladies at an hour best suited for their convenience, namely 3pm'. The first subject was *The Elements of Chemistry*, followed by further courses in 1871 in Astronomy, Botany and the Atmosphere. All were well attended and the examiner thought the class well qualified to study a scientific subject. In 1882 'Twelve Lessons for Ladies' were presented on Political Economy including Productive and Unproductive Labour, Wages, Profits, Rent, Value, the Currency, Foreign Trade, Taxation. The lectures were attended by 90 students who achieved very good results in the written examination.

In the 1879–80 season classes on various subjects were started: elocution and discussion, chess, natural history, chemistry, physics, shorthand and vocal music. Ladies were offered morning classes in German and French and a Saturday morning class in drawing and painting. The art class continued for the next fourteen years, but the other classes tended to fade out.

Most of these classes required a fee and the teachers were paid. This was certainly so in the case of twelve lessons offered in 1884 by Karl Marx's youngest daughter, Eleanor, on the study of Shakespeare's *As You Like It*.

Highgate Literary & Scientific Institution.

THE READING AND STUDY OF

SHAKSPERE.

PROPOSED CLASS

FOR THE STUDY OF

"AS YOU LIKE IT,"

UNDER THE DIRECTION OF

ELEANOR MARX.

The Comedy will be read by the members of the Class. Difficult references, archaic forms, and the dramatic construction of the play will be explained and discussed. Students are advised to obtain the Clarendon Press Edition of " As You Like It " (Macmillan, price 1/6).

("As You Like It" is the Play selected for the Cambridge Higher Local Examinations of June, 1884.)

Fee for the course of 12 lessons £1 1s., if ten names are entered, apply to LIBRARIAN.

Other Classes for the Study of Elocution and Literature can be formed by arrangement.

The handbill states that the course required ten pupils at a fee of 21/-. It is not certain that the course took place but as the play was the one selected for the Cambridge Higher Local Examinations of June 1884 there is every likelihood that it did.

From 1880 until 1885 special educational courses of eight lectures, with written examinations at the end, were given on alternating scientific and literary subjects. These were successfully revived between 1892 and 1899 as University Extension Lectures.

Ninety years later, in 1989, educational courses returned with a series on local history, run by the University of London Centre for Extra-Mural Studies.

Literary activities, including poetry and prose readings, were popular in the nineteenth and early twentieth centuries. A highlight was the reading by Charles Dickens Jnr from his father's works on 5 January 1892. Nearly 100 years later, on 31 January 1989 a *Charles Dickens Evening* consisted of readings from Dickens by actor residents of Highgate – David Swift, Tim Pigott-Smith, Paul Rogers, Pamela Miles, Rosalind Boxall and Paula Jacobs. The same group of actors gave readings from the novels and letters of George Eliot in October 1989, all going to prove that modern taste is not so very different from that of the nineteenth century.

Readings from plays made an auspicious start in 1845; Charles Kemble was engaged to give three Shakespearean readings in December of that year and another in 1846. His daughter Mrs Butler (née Fanny Kemble) gave three more readings in 1848. Occasional play-readings continued until the end of the century but interest in drama lapsed until 1938, only to be curtailed by the outbreak of war. Further play-reading groups were started for time to time, but most lapsed for lack of sustained enthusiasm. Most of the drama events were presented by outside groups.

An Institution Theatre Group was formed in 1989 to visit plays, opera and ballet.

DISCUSSIONS, DEBATES, QUIZZES

In November 1848 a Mutual Improvement Class was started which was to all intents and purposes a debating society. Topics such as the following were debated:

'Is the mental capacity of the sexes equal?'

'Is emigration beneficial to the community at large?'

Not until 1882 did the Institution's Debating Society proper begin under the presidency of F.L. Soper. The Society held ten debates during the first season. Of outstanding interest must have been the one on 10 November 'That the exclusion of Women from the Parliamentary Franchise is indefensible'. Although the proposer and the opposer were men the handbill invited all members, associates and friends, and said that ladies were particularly welcome and asked to speak. Indeed it was advertised that two ladies from the Central Committee of the National Society for Women's Suffrage would take part.

Some quizzes were organised in the 1950s, but none approached the

29. *The Institution's Centenary Dinner at the Criterion Restaurant, Piccadilly, on 16 January 1939.*

30. *The Victorian Ball held to celebrate the centenary of the building of the Lecture Hall in 1980. Left to right: Mrs Christina Giles (wife of the Headmaster of Highgate School), Mrs Loveday Fowler, Mrs Barbara Edwards, Edward Fowler (President of HLSI), Mrs Jean Pateman (Chairman of the Friends of Highgate Cemetery), John Pateman (Hon. Sec. HLSI), and Mrs Gwynydd Gosling (Librarian).*

stature of the Grand Quiz, an intellectual contest between the Highgate Society and the Institution. This was initiated in the 1970–71 season and has continued ever since as a successful annual activity. For the third Grand Quiz Isla Merry donated the 'Isla Merry Mug' for the winner.

Recently (1989–90) two literary circles (day and evening) have been organised which meet once a month to discuss a novel or other literary work of the group's choice.

LITERARY DINNERS

Inaugurated in Autumn 1984, the literary dinners now constitute one of the most important Institution activities. Books signed by the authors are on sale. The success of the first dinner merited a second in the Spring. Dinners (often Spring and Autumn) have followed on an irregular basis ever since. Speakers have included Donald Sinden, Bernard Levin, Elizabeth Longford, Melvyn Bragg, Simon Brett, Sally Burton and Denis Healey.

Many other events also take place: the celebration of anniversaries, twice-yearly antiques fairs, auctions, food fairs, book fairs and Christmas Bazaars. Could anyone deny that Highgate, without the Institution, would be a much duller place?

31. Masked Ball held at Channing School, Highgate, on May 20 1989, as part of the Institution's 150th Anniversary Celebrations.

CHAPTER EIGHT

Village Links

Use of Premises by Outside Organisations or Persons

A number of societies flourish in Highgate – among them the Highgate Society, the Highgate Horticultural Society and the Highgate Choral Society. All of them make some use of the Institution's premises. The Highgate Society, which was formed in 1966 out of an environmental group known as the Save Highgate Committee, is housed in 10A South Grove. Many members of the Institution also belong to the Highgate Society and the Horticultural Society, which was founded in 1859.

This Chapter gives some account of the use made by other Village societies of the Institution's lecture hall; there are also lettings to individuals.

The earliest record of the use of the Institution premises by an outside organisation is found in a Minute dated February 1852 stating that the United Provident Association used a room for their society's meetings two evenings a month and the cost was four shillings per meeting. In the years before World War I the Highgate District Nursing Association, the North London Working Girls' Guild, and the British and Foreign Bible Society (Highgate Ancillary) all held meetings regularly. The Santa Claus Society hired the Hall in autumn 1907 for their annual exhibition of dolls intended as gifts for children in the London Hospital, and this 'Dolls Show' became an annual event until 1931.

During the years of the First World War the Institution premises were used for various purposes connected with the War. The SPCA (now RSPCA) held a sale in 1916 for horses wounded in the War. The Highgate Company of the Eastern Command Volunteer Ambulance Convoy held their annual meetings to appeal for funds in 1917 and 1918. The Highgate War Hospital's annual meeting was held in the Hall in 1917 and so was a meeting for the Hornsey Prisoners of War Fund. In December 1917 and December 1918 the Hall was used for concerts for wounded soldiers.

Gentler pursuits returned in the post-war period. The Highgate Chrysanthemum Society, the Wireless Society of Highgate, the League of Nations Union, the Highgate Poetry Society, all met regularly in the 1920s and 30s. There was also drama in 1930. In 1938 the Hall was used for ARP lectures and as a depot for storing gas masks. More than 2000 people received their gas masks here.

After the War the use of the Hall by outside bodies became more intense and varied. The Highgate Choral Society used the Hall from 1963–1971 for autumn and winter rehearsals. In 1964 a Keep Fit class was arranged through the Kentish Town Institute of the L.C.C., which continued for three winters. The Highgate Horticultural Society has used the Institution premises for its Annual Spring Show since 1966, its Annual Autumn Show since 1987 and its Annual General Meeting since 1981. The Highgate Society used and continues to use the Hall for many purposes: Annual General Meetings, Archway Road Meetings, Burns' Night Suppers, Valentine Celebrations, Exhibitions, readings by Highgate poets and so on.

The Medau Rhythmic Movement Group used the Hall regularly for classes from 1967 to 1983. The National Association of Decorative and Fine Arts Societies (Highgate Branch) held meetings from 1975–77 and again from 1984. The Gatehouse Theatre used the Hall for rehearsals occasionally from 1976. Institution premises were used for Blood Donor sessions twice yearly from 1976 to 1984.

Since 1969 there have been many wedding receptions. From 1980 the diversity of organisations using the Institution's facilities increased. There were Slimnastics, The Portfolio Society held a meeting, there were concerts, an embroidery group, singers, talks on photography, a tennis club party. The North West Middlesex Beekeepers' Association continues to hold its Annual General Meeting, as do six Residents' Associations and the Friends of Highgate Cemetery. Meetings take place of the directors of the Harington Scheme which was created by voluntary effort to train young people with learning difficulties, from the two boroughs of Haringey and Islington (hence the name), in gardening skills and to assist them to find employment. There are fetes, lunch parties, birthday parties, wine tastings and many one-off bookings.

Organisations and individuals hiring the Institution for teaching has a long tradition. In 1844 Mademoiselle Panormo had the use of the Lecture Hall and Committee Room to give singing lessons. According to a handbill there was a middle-class cookery course of ten lessons on Saturday mornings, costing 21 shillings. A more recent example is the series of lectures on European Art given in 1985–86 for the wives of Japanese businessmen.

An interesting feature of the Institution's history has been the way it has generated other groups and societies. The earliest example was the Microscopical and Natural History Society, which started life as a class in 1880. A society which still flourishes is the Highgate Choral Society, which was first established in 1888 within the Institution.

Finally a summary table of the hire of the Institution premises by other organisations or persons for the years 1987, 1988 and 1989 is presented below. This gives some idea of the busy life of the Institution apart from the many diverse activities of or on behalf of its members. In addition, the diaries for these three years show a considerable number of visitors and students.

SUMMARY TABLE

Hire of Premises by Outside Organisations or Persons

1987		1988		1989	
Social		**Social**		**Social**	
Lunch Party	1	Lunch	1	Rotary Ladies Evening	1
Evening Party	1	Parties	4	Golden Wedding Lunch	1
Xmas Party	1	Wedding Reception	1	Wedding Receptions	2
Wedding Receptions	2	Ruby Wedding	1	Soirée with Christies	1
Ruby Wedding	1	Reception after Service	1	Party	1
After Funeral Receptions	2	Dinner Dance	1	Tea	1
Meetings		**Meetings**		**Meetings**	
NADFAS	1 day	NADFAS	5 days	NADFAS	3 x ½days
	½ day		2 mornings		4 mornings
	5 mornings	St Michael's Church	1	North Middx Beekeepers	5
Highgate Society		Kingsley Place		Hill Homes	1
Transport	1	Neighbourhood Watch	1	Horticultural Society	2
Camden Enquiry	2 days	Antique Collectors	1	Highgate Society	1
Highgate Society	2	Apollo House Residents'		Cholmeley Lodge	
South Grove House		Association	1	Residents' Association	1
Residents' Association	3	South Grove House		South Grove House	
Cholmeley Lodge		Residents' Association	1	Residents' Association	1
Residents' Association	1	Highgate Society	1		
Apollo House Residents'		N.W. London Architects	1		
Association	1	Horticultural Society	3		
Action Aid	1	Harington Scheme	1		
Highgate Cemetery	1	North Middx Beekeepers	4		
Miscellaneous		**Miscellaneous**		**Miscellaneous**	
Twinlight Trail	10 weekends	Twinlight Trail	8 x 3 days	Twinlight Trail	2 x 3 days
Horticultural Society Spring			1 x 4 days		4 x 6 days
and Autumn Shows	2	Horticultural Society Spring			1 x 5 days
Calibre Fair	1	and Autumn Shows	2 days	Horticultural Society Spring	
Highgate Choral Society		Camden History Society		and Autumn shows	2 days
Rehearsal	1	Lectures	2	Highgate Society Lecture	1
Antiques Market	1	Calibre Sale	2 days	Camden History Society	
Poetry Reading	1	WPI Summer School Play	4 days	Lecture	1
City of London Orchestra		Dr Barnado's Antique		Antiques Market	2 days
Rehearsal	1	Road Show	1	Gatehouse Theatre Club	4 days
		Antique Markets	4 days	Highgate Choral Society	
		Poetry Evening	1	Rehearsal	1
		Turkish Painting			
		Exhibition	1		
		Turkish Carpets	2 days		
		Highgate Society			
		Craft Fair	1		

CHAPTER NINE

Presidents and Personalities

People distinguished in many walks of life have contributed to the success of the Institution. The Appendix contains lists of all the Presidents, Secretaries and Librarians and the following pages contain profiles of a few of the more colourful personalities – or 'Highgate Worthies'. J.H. Lloyd's comment on them is apt: 'Living on a hill famed for its bracing air, the inhabitants seem to be endowed with a kind of Highland vigour both bodily and mentally'.

HARRY CHESTER (1808–1868)

Harry Chester was Chairman of the Inaugural Meeting and then President of the Institution from 1839–1856. From Highgate's privileged class – his father, Sir Robert Chester, lived in The Old Hall, and his own home was the Queen Anne South Grove House (now superseded by a block of flats) – he wanted the advantages he enjoyed to be far more widely spread than was the early Victorian norm. Educated at Westminster School and Trinity College, Cambridge, he entered the Civil Service as a Clerk to the Privy Council.

32. Harry Chester (1808–68), first President of the HLSI (1839–56).

His interests extended far beyond the Institution. Other local activities engaged his interest including 'allotment gardening for the labouring poor'. Thanks also to his industry Highgate Village ceased to have to put up with cattle drovers passing through the Village on Sundays on their way to Monday markets in the metropolis.

Education proved an abiding passion. In the Privy Council his main work was on its Education Committee where he was officially responsible for paying building grants for which plans had to be submitted. His pamphlet *Hints on the building and management of schools* contains the plan of a slow-burning 'Chester stove' and goes on: 'The school room should be as comfortable and pleasing to the eye as possible, with a few good bright maps, a few good diagrams, a few well-chosen texts on the walls. Texts such as "Our God is a consuming fire" and "All liars shall burn in the lake that burneth with fire and brimstone" are to be avoided. The school should provide washing facilities, but not on a large scale as the children should come to the school with clean hands. There should also be small gardens, a pigsty, rabbit hutches, beehives, hen runs and a wash-house and laundry. The children should be encouraged to make and classify a natural history section, learn drawing and have the opportunity of practising music, vocal and instrumental.'

Highgate benefited from his educational interests as he secured a large grant from the Privy Council Committee towards the building of the National School in North Road in 1850 (now St Michael's School). Chester was also Treasurer and a Governor of Highgate School.

In the Royal Society of Arts (of which he became a vice-president) he saw a way of advancing adult education. Thanks to Chester in 1851 various adult education institutions throughout the country became affiliated to the RSA and an examination system developed which is still widely used today. By the mid–1850s he was devoting much of his time to the RSA and resigned as the Institution's President, although he remained an honorary member of the organisation he had so successfully launched.

33. Professor Charles Tomlinson (1808–97), President of HLSI 1876–77. One of the prime movers in the regeneration of the Institution 1879–80.

CHARLES TOMLINSON (1808–1897)

Charles Tomlinson was a self-taught man who became a Professor in Experimental Science at King's College, London, and a Fellow of the Royal Society. As a young man he had various unrewarding clerical jobs and his life was only made bearable by his attendance at evening lectures in Physics and Chemistry at the Birkbeck Institution.

In 1830 Tomlinson and his brother opened a school in Salisbury, where he taught modern languages and experimental science. He married in Salisbury and in 1842 he and his wife Sarah moved to London. He wrote many papers for scientific magazines and in the mid–40s he was appointed to a lectureship at King's College. From that time the Tomlinsons lived in Hampstead until they came to 7 North Road in Highgate in 1866.

Tomlinson joined the Institution and was soon made Honorary Secretary, an office which he held from 1867–1876. During this time the fortunes of the Institution were at a low ebb and he came to an arrangement with the Working Men's Club to combine their resources – the Working Men's Club was in want of a room and the Institution was often in want of an audience. On his resignation as Secretary when he was approaching seventy he was asked to be President and accepted the appointment for just one year, 1876–77. He then became Treasurer of the Rebuilding Fund, which was very successful and the renovated building was ready for opening in 1880.

During his thirty years' association with the Institution Professor Tomlinson lectured on a variety of subjects which included 'Fermentation', 'On the Leading Idea of Dante's *Comedy*', 'The Science of a Tea Kettle', 'Faraday', 'Benjamin Franklin and the Lightning Conductor' and 'Sir John Franklin in the Arctic Region'. He set himself a vigorous programme of lectures and also invited friends of his from King's College to give lectures at the Institution; in return, to save fees, he gave lectures to them.

His favourite hobby was chess and he soon had a flourishing Chess Club at the Institution as well as having frequent evenings at his home for 'Chess, Tobacco and Conversation'. He was the life of intellectual gatherings in Highgate. His wife Sarah formed a reading circle of half a dozen families who could 'come together at regular intervals for a rational and social evening without formality or great preparation. The gentlemen read aloud from standard works – the ladies served! Simplicity was the order of the day and woe betide any lady who put jellies and cream on the table for refreshment.'

In 1891 Professor Tomlinson lectured at the Institution for the last time. He was due to speak again in 1892, but bad weather prevented his attending and his lecture 'On knowing something well' was printed for distribution to members. This was the end of his active association with the Institution, but he remained intellectually active, despite increasing blindness and ill-health, to the end of his life in 1897.

THE BARONESS BURDETT-COUTTS (1814–1906)

Baroness Angela Burdett-Coutts, who owned Holly Lodge, Highgate, from 1837 until her death in 1906, joined the Institution in 1862 and was a member for forty-four years.

She subscribed generously to the fund for the rebuilding of 1879–1880 and took a close interest in the Institution's programmes. For example, the Annual Report for 1875 records that when the lecture list for 1884–85 was circulated she pointed out that there was no lecture on 'the great scientific event of the year, namely the transit of Venus', and proposed that a supplementary lecture be given. She invited Mr W. Pengelly of Torquay to deliver the lecture, which was given on 21 January 1875 to a full audience, and she herself was present. She opened the new Lecture Hall at an impressive ceremony in 1880: 'The newly erected Lecture Hall had a platform at one end covered with crimson baize overlaid with a Brussels carpet; the large double doors from the entrance hall were hung with crimson baize curtains on brass rails...'

The Baroness was the daughter of Sir Francis Burdett, the Radical M.P. Her great fortune came to her from her maternal grandfather Thomas Coutts. He had installed Harriot Mellon, who was to become his second wife, in Holly Lodge before his first wife's death and left her his entire fortune. It was she who made Angela Burdett her heir on condition that she added Coutts to her name and so the shareholding in Coutts' bank, the house at 1 Stratton Street as well as Holly Lodge came into her possession.

She was a serious-minded girl who inherited her great wealth at the age of 23 and decided to devote it to charity, or philanthropy as it was then called. She did not want to be famous for her giving and would often appear on subscription lists as 'Lady Unknown', which became the title of Edna Healey's biography. Charles Dickens directed her charitable giving for a number of years and said of her that 'she saw with kind eyes'. Her special interests were the Ragged Schools, the building of a block of flats for poor families in Columbia Square and a new (and unsuccessful) market hall nearby in Bethnal Green, the building of St Stephen's Church, Westminster, a Home for Fallen Women, and missionary expeditions including Livingstone's. One of her most practical gifts was a drying machine – on which 1,000 garments could be thoroughly dried in 25 minutes – which she had sent to Florence Nightingale in the Crimean War; Dickens wrote that the machine was 'the solitary "administrative" thing connected with the War that had been a success'.

But the many charitable works of Angela Burdett-Coutts did not pass unnoticed. Philanthropy on such a vast scale could not be performed in

34. *Baroness Burdett-Coutts (1814–1906), philanthropist granddaughter of Thomas Coutts, the banker, whose fortune she inherited. Her home at Holly Lodge was the scene of many distinguished gatherings and its beautiful gardens were the venue for shows of the Highgate Horticultural Society. The Baroness attended the grand reopening of the HLSI after the rebuilding of 1880.*

secret. In 1871 Queen Victoria raised Angela to the peerage under the title of Baroness Burdett-Coutts of Highgate and Brookfield, Middlesex. No other woman had ever had such an honour conferred on her in recognition of her own deeds.

At Holly Lodge the Baroness entertained many prominent statesmen, writers, bishops and explorers. Not all her guests were famous. She greeted many parties of East End schoolchildren at the entrance on West Hill. At one school party in 1866 'two hundred and sixteen pottles of strawberries were eaten' (a pottle was a small wicker basket).

She numbered among her friends the Duke of Wellington, Disraeli, Gladstone, Florence Nightingale, General Gordon, Livingstone and Henry Irving. At the age of 68 she made what the Queen characterised as 'her mad marriage' to a young man, Ashmead Bartlett, forty years her junior. In 1885 he became Conservative Member of Parliament for Westminster and introduced into the House of Commons what became the Hampstead Heath Act which preserved Parliament Hill and three hundred acres of Hampstead Heath as an open space.

The Baroness died in 1906 at the age of 92 at her house in Stratton Street; 25,000 people filed past her coffin there, a last salutation to the 'Queen of the Poor'. She was buried in Westminster Abbey; on her coffin at the end were only the Queen's lilies and her husband's posy of sweet herbs from 'the Garden on the Hill'.

JOHN HENRY LLOYD (1830–1910)

John Henry Lloyd became a member of the Institution in 1871, was elected to the Committee of Management in 1874 and became successively Hon. Secretary (1875–93), Hon. Treasurer (1893–1900) and Vice-President (1900–1910). Although he was never President he was one of the saviours of the Institution. When he joined, the fortunes of the Institution were again at a very low ebb and closure seemed likely when the lease expired. Lloyd persuaded the Committee not only to remain in business but to expand, and as Secretary he negotiated the renewal of the lease with an 'unwilling landlord' and launched the campaign for the rebuilding programme of 1879–80. As a personal contribution he wrote *The History, Topography and Antiquities of Highgate*, 500 copies of which were subscribed for and the whole of the surplus was presented to the library for the purchase of 4,000 books.

Lloyd was a member of a firm of wine merchants, H.R. Williams & Co., who had their business at Crosby Hall in the City. When he came to Highgate he lived first at Hillside, Jackson's Lane, from which, despite the newly completed Great Eastern Railway line nearby, he rode daily on horseback to the office. He later moved to Greenbank, Merton Lane, which had several acres of gardens, paddocks and field, and here he established a small farm. Finally he moved to The Grove (no. 10), regarding it as 'the hub of Highgate'.

He played an important part in the affairs of the Village. He belonged to the Highgate Congregational Church, of which he was Secretary and

35. John Henry Lloyd (1830–1910). He, with Professor Tomlinson, was chiefly involved in the rebuilding of 1879–80. He wrote his History and Antiquities of Highgate *in 1888, for the 50th anniversary of the Institution the following year.*

Treasurer for many years. He assisted his business colleague, H.R. Williams, in saving the Highgate Woods. He had a unique collection of sketches of old Highgate and presented many prints and drawings, including a set of Hogarth engravings, to the Institution.

He introduced many lecturers to the Institution and he himself gave four talks, including one on *Highgate and some of its Worthies* and another on *Caenwood and its Historical Associations*.

ROBERT STEWART WHIPPLE (1871–1953)

Robert Whipple was one of the great benefactors of the Institution. He was President from 1937 to 1953 and during that time reorganised the administration of the Institution as well as helping to solve its financial problems out of his own pocket.

He was an important figure in the world of scientific instruments and his collection of instruments and books formed the nucleus of the Whipple Museum of the History of Science at Cambridge University, which was inaugurated in 1951. The 1,500 volumes include first editions of the works of Gilbert, Bacon, Galileo, Boyle, Hooke and Newton; the specimens include astronomical instruments from the sixteenth century onwards.

36. *Robert Stewart Whipple (1871–1953), President of the Institution from 1937– 53. It was due to his generosity and organising skill that the Institution survived its financial crisis after the Second World War.*

After leaving King's College School, Wimbledon in 1888 he joined the staff of Kew Observatory, of which his father was Superintendent. In his *Reminiscences of an Instrument Maker*, published in 1942, he describes his first job which was to help in calculating the velocity and height of clouds by means of two cameras placed half-a-mile apart with two observers communicating with each other by telephone; in this way he was in at the birth of the telecommunications industry. He was the first employee of Dr Horace Darwin, son of Charles Darwin, in what later became the Cambridge Scientific & Technology Instrument Company. The Whipple-Darwin connection was exemplified in Dr Wilma George's 1989 Whipple Trust lecture on Darwin.

Whipple went on to hold high office in a number of scientific associations and learned societies including the Scientific Instrument Manufacturers' Association, the Optical Society, the Institute of Physics, of which he was a founder member, and the Physical Society; he was Faraday Lecturer of the Institute of Electrical Engineers.

He came to Highgate, where he lived at 6 Old Hall, in 1927 and soon became involved in the affairs of the Institution. He was elected President in 1937 and both before and after the Second World War played an active part: even when he was, through illness, absent for some time during the War the Management Committee did not think anyone else could be considered for the Presidency.

After the War the membership and finances of the Institution needed rebuilding. He personally redeemed the Loan Stock, which enabled the Institution to continue without a heavy load of debt and gave it the unencumbered freehold ownership of its property. Without this act of generosity the Institution could not have survived.

His last gift, which was made shortly before he died, was the endowment of the Robert Whipple Trust 'for the furtherance of literature, science and the arts in North London': the Whipple Lecture given annually at the Institution is financed from the Trust, which also gives £50 per annum to the Archives Committee.

Sir James Brown (1892–1979)

37. Sir James Raitt Brown (1892–1979), President of the Institution 1953–73. His great enthusiasm for local history led him to put in order the Institution's archives.

Sir James Brown was one of the most distinguished of the Institution's Presidents. Educated at Merchant Taylors' School, he joined the staff of the then Ecclesiastical Commissioners in 1912 as a junior clerk. After serving in the First World War he returned to the Commissioners, becoming Secretary in 1937. During this period he laid the foundations of the encyclopaedic knowledge of the history and affairs of the Commissioners, which enabled him in 1946–7 to play a leading role in the merger with Queen Anne's Bounty; this led to the creation of the present Church Commissioners. The union and the foundation of the new body corporate was a major administrative task and in recognition of this he was knighted in 1948. In 1954 he retired from the office of Secretary and became Third Church Estates Commissioner at the invitation of Archbishop Fisher. In 1963 the Archbishop conferred on him the degree of LLD.

Sir James, who lived in Southwood Lawn Road, joined the Institution in 1938, the Committee of Management in 1940 and was elected President in 1953. During his Presidency the Institution profited greatly from his wide administrative experience; he was determined to see the Institution firmly supported on a sound financial base and growing membership. He strengthened the Committee of Management by bringing in members with wide talents and experience. He helped to establish the Robert Whipple Trust which provides a lecture of high calibre each year, and the Edith Ellen Harris Trust which contributes annually many valuable non-fiction books to the Library. He gave enthusiastic support to the building up of the Archives material and bequeathed his own writings and the results of his researches to the Institution.

Above all, it was his personal qualities that endeared him to members of the Institution and to the people of Highgate and made him such an influential figure. The Annual Report of 1974 said of him: 'He is an excellent speaker and his delightful wit has refreshed many an Institution occasion and has added to what is one of his most fascinating gifts, not only to the Institution but also to all the people of Highgate – his profound and scholarly knowledge of the history of the neighbourhood'. He was also famous for his conducted walks which were 'full of interesting information, anecdote and witty comment'.

He gave many talks on Highgate – its history, people and buildings. They were presented with scholarship, humour and a vivid historical imagination. For instance, his account of the young Queen Victoria's runaway coach on Highgate West Hill depicts the alarm of the young footman who hoped 'Old Saddlebags knows what he's doing'. *Once on a Mayday Morning* describes the procession of the Lord Mayor and aldermen of the City riding out to meet the new King James I on his way to London on 1 May 1604: 'The Lord Mayor and the aldermen have arrived in their silk and fur-trimmed gowns, and with them have come riding out from the City 500 of London's leading citizens. They are indeed a sight to be gaped at and ever-remembered, with their plumed caps and fine cloths, some in silk-slashed doublets, some in the gowns of their guilds or companies, all on fine horses richly caparisoned.'

Another example of Sir James's gift for conjuring a scene from Highgate's past is his account of Queen Victoria's coronation dinner: 'Over 1,200 people were to sit down together to a dinner in North Street (as the North Road was then called) and tables 900 feet long were erected from near the Gatehouse to the yard of the Castle Inn. In fact June was hay-making time and in those days all the fields were meadows – hay was a most important crop in those horse-drawn times – and every year whole families came out from London slums to cut the hay by hand. They used to camp in the fields till the hay had been laid.

'In 1838 there were 1,000 of them. They demanded invitations and nearly doubled the party, which got through 1208lbs of roast beef, 610lbs of bread, 870lbs of potatoes, 121 plum puddings of 9lbs each, 350 cabbages and 1,600 pints of porter.'

Sir James did a great deal of research into the lives of men who had founded or built up the Village, and when he recounted their stories he would put an amusing twist on them. For instance at a meeting of the Hornsey Historical Society he described Highgate's founders as a hermit, a philanthropic vintner, an illegitimate son of a Yorkshire squire and a leper. William Phelipe was the real founder of Highgate; he was a hermit who brought water to Highgate by digging a dew pond and he got authority from the king, via the bishop, to build a road into London. William Blake, a vintner, built the fine 17th-century houses in The Grove and planned to build a school for the poor children of the City, but his creditors grew impatient and he ended his life in Newgate debtors' prison. Highgate School was founded by Roger Cholmondley, the illegitimate son of a York-shire squire. William Pole, a leper and a captain in Edward IV's army, was allowed to build a lazar home and this was Highgate's first hospital. Finally he mentioned Thomas Collett who in the 17th century drew up the first planning scheme for Highgate, and evidence of this can still be seen in Pond Square.

Sir James was a member of St Michael's church where he served as church-warden. From his war service he became interested in Toc H and was a member of the Highgate branch, which in those days met in 10A. In 1967 he played a prominent part in founding the Highgate Society, of which he was a Vice-President. He was also President of the Camden History Society and a member of the Athenaeum.

He had wit and charm as well as scholarship, and many people have paid tribute to his kindness in all matters, however trivial. His modesty was captured in *Buzz* of June 1978 which described an attempt to interview him. 'Catch Him at his gate before he disappears behind the pink crab apple blossom, solicit him for some venture promising personal limelight and he'll dismiss the notion politely but brusquely."No, no", he'll say, "not me, I'm not really important. I don't matter".'

*38. Dame Geraldine
Aves (1899–1986).
Involved in the
Institution in many
capacities from 1955
until her death, and
founder of the Archives
Committee in 1976.*

DAME GERALDINE AVES (1899–1986)

Dame Geraldine Aves was another of the Institution's most distinguished members.

Some three years after graduating from Newnham College, Cambridge in 1920, Geraldine Aves joined the School Care Committee Service of the London County Council. In 1938 she went to County Hall to help plan the evacuation of London's school children in the event of war. By 1941 her experience with childcare and other problems that the War and the evacuation scheme had brought, led to her secondment from the L.C.C. to the then Ministry of Health.

At the end of the War she became for 15 months the Chief Child Care Consultant for Europe to the United Nations Relief and Rehabilitation Administration (UNRRA), the first international relief agency in world history. In 1951 she went to the United Nations to set up the Family and Child Welfare Unit of the newly created UN Division of Social Welfare. In 1952 she returned to her by now established position as the first Chief Welfare Officer at the Ministry of Health, a post she held until her retirement, playing a unique role in the development of social welfare services.

After her retirement in 1963 Dame Geraldine continued to influence social policy but increasingly in the voluntary field. In 1966 she was appointed Chairman of a Working Party, known as the Aves Committee, set up to enquire into the use of voluntary workers in the Social Service. The Aves Report (*The Voluntary Worker in the Social Services*) was published in 1969 and led to the creation of a national organisation, The Volunteer Centre.

Other organisations of which she was either founder-member, governor, president, chairman or trustee, were the Council for Training in Social Work, the National Institute for Social Work Training, the Advisory Council of the National Council for the Care of Old People, the London Diocesan Synod and Bishop's Council, the North London Hospice and Manor Gardens Centre in North Islington. She was active in Newnham College affairs throughout her life and was a made a Fellow in 1981. She received the DBE in 1977.

Dame Geraldine was also a commanding figure in the local community, and became Chairman and later Trustee of the Highgate Cemetery Trust and a member of both the Community Service and Environment Committee of the Highgate Society.

Perhaps her most outstanding contribution to Highgate was the initiative she took from her base in the Highgate Society to found the Harington Scheme, a horticultural training scheme for young people with serious learning difficulties. This scheme exemplified her belief in the importance of combining voluntary effort with statutory support and charitable finances.

Despite her many varied commitments, Dame Geraldine, who lived in Highgate for 54 years, found time to serve the Institution and was a member from 1955 until her death in 1986 at the age of 87. She was Chairman of the Library Committee from 1973 to 1977 and in that capacity set up its Archives Working Party in 1976. She was a member of the Management Committee from 1972 until 1976, when she became a Vice-President, an office which she held until her death.

Into The Future

Immediately after the celebrations of its one hundred and fiftieth anniversary the Institution turned its attention to preparing itself for the twenty-first century. The buildings of the Institution had had no major improvements for over one hundred years and the fabric and structure had become dangerously unsound in a number of places: the Librarian's flat was in need of total renovation and, most significantly, the Library had become so overcrowded that many books were inaccessible to all but the most determined and agile. Plans were therefore put in hand for the launching in January 1990 of a major fund-raising programme and work started on the structural repairs and improvements to the building as a whole in April 1990.

Members have responded most generously to the appeal and, as had happened before at critical junctures in the Institution's history, the need to raise money for rebuilding stimulated more activities and an increase in membership. It is hoped that work on restoring and improving the premises will be completed by 1992, except for the Library for which funds are still urgently required, and the Institution looks forward to playing a key role in the social and cultural life of Highgate in the next century.

'Enough; and leave the rest to Fame!'

From *An Epitaph* by Andrew Marvell (1621–78).

39. 'Andrew Marvell's Cottage' on Highgate Hill. According to Marvell's own letters he was living in Highgate in 1675; at the same time his political enemy, the Earl of Lauderdale, was in possession of Lauderdale House. What is thought to be Marvell's home was this cottage, situated a few yards from Lauderdale House, nearer the Village, but there is no documentary evidence to support the strong legend.

ANDREW MARVEL'S HOUSE,
HIGHGATE.
DEMOLISHED 1868.

Appendix

PRESIDENTS

Harry Chester	1839–1858
William Gladstone	1858–1866
Rev. John Bradley Dyne	1866–1867
Sir William Henry Bodkin (Judge)	1867–1868
Lt. Col. Josiah Wilkinson	1868–1869
Sir Sydney Hedley Waterlow	1869–1870
W.H. Michael, Q.C.	1870–1871
James Brotherton – died in office (W.P. Bodkin acted)	
Edward Fry, Q.C.	1872–1873
Col. Leach	1873–1874
Benjamin G. Lake	1874–1876
Charles Tomlinson	1876–1877
William Green	1877–1878
The Rev. Andrew Jukes, M.A.	1878–1880
The Hon. Mr Justice Fry (becoming 'The Rt. Hon. Lord Justice'	1880–1884
William Peter Bodkin	1884–1886
J. Glover, J.P.	1886–1887
Col. Josiah Wilkinson	1887–1888
A.S. Harvey	1888–1890
J.B. Dyne	1890–1891
Arthur Marshall	1891–1892
John Sime	1892–1893
Dr. Harry Greenwood	1893–1895
Abram Lyle	1895–1896
Percival Hart	1896–1897
Walter Reynolds, J.P.	1897–1900
Harry W. Birks	1900–1913
James Anderson	1913–1915
David Croal Thomson	1915–1919
Sir Bignell Elliott	1919–1924

W.H. Gillett	1924–1925
Dr. A.E.C. Dickinson	1925–1928
John Ravenshaw	1928–1930
Harold Wade	1930–1932
Sir Bignell Elliott	1932–1933
Frederick J. Varley	1933–1937
Robert Stewart Whipple	1937–1953
Sir James Brown	1953–1973
Edward Fowler	1973–1981
Peter Benton	1981–1988
Judge Quentin Edwards	1988

HONORARY SECRETARIES

Rev. Robert Carter Smith	1839–1848
James Beaumont	1848–1849
J.S. Godfrey	1849–1856
W.P. Bodkin	1856–1866
Charles Tomlinson	1866–1876
John Henry Lloyd	1876–1893
Frederic Hamilton Crowdy	1893–1925
Cora Hale	1926–1935
Ivor Idris	1936–1937
G. Wilfrid Davis	1938–1958
Beatrix Goodman	1958–1962
Kathleen Budgett-Meakin	1962–1979
John Pateman	1979–1985
Elizabeth Fletcher	1985–1986
Neil Barnes	1986-

HONORARY LIBRARIANS

Charles Empson	1890–1909
Chairman of Library Committee	1910–1912
Rev. S.B. Simons, M.A.	1913–1918
Dr. A.E.C. Dickinson	1923–1928
Donald Mackenzie	1928–1929
Geoffrey Hawke	–1939

LIBRARIANS

G.W. Davies	1839–1844
Richard Whitmore and wife	1844–1859
Mr Noakes	1859–1860
Charles Noakes (son)	1860
Charles Lee	1860–1875
John Snow	1875–1878
Charles Benson Scott and mother	1878–1882
James Drummond and wife	1882–1895
Henry Holt and wife	1895–1903
Alfred Holmes and wife and daughter	1903–1929
J.P. Wilson and wife	1929–1934
George Taylor	1934–1936
Mr Chapman	1936–1937
Mrs Brunton	1937–1939
Mrs Hurst	1937–1940
Elaine Vaughan	1939–1968
Miss Gliksten (assistant)	1940–1941
Iris Pyemont (assistant)	1941–1968
Gwynydd Gosling	1968–1990

INDEX

Entries in bold type refer to illustrations